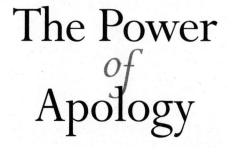

The Power
of
Apology

Also by Beverly Engel:

The Right to Innocence

Divorcing a Parent

The Emotionally Abused Woman

Encouragements for the Emotionally Abused Woman

Partners in Recovery

Familes in Recovery

Raising Your Sexual Self-Esteem

Beyond the Birds and the Bees

Blessings from the Fall

The Parenthood Decision

Sensual Sex

Loving Him without Losing You

Women Circling the Earth

The Power *of* Apology

Healing Steps to Transform All Your Relationships

BEVERLY ENGEL

John Wiley & Sons, Inc.

New York • Chichester • Weinheim • Brisbane • Singapore • Toronto

Published by John Wiley & Sons, Inc.

Published simultaneously in Canada

Design and production by Navta Associates, Inc.

This publication is designed to provide accurate and authoritative information in regard to the subject matter covered. It is sold with the understanding that the publisher is not engaged in rendering professional services. If professional advice or other expert assistance is required, the services of a competent professional person should be sought.

With the exception of public figures or those cited in the media, the names and identifying characteristics of everyone in this book have been changed to protect their confidentiality.

Library of Congress Cataloging-in-Publication Data:

Engel, Beverly.
    The power of apology : healing steps to transform all your relationships / Beverly Engel.
      p. cm.
    Includes bibliographical references and index.
    ISBN 0-471-39907-8 (alk. paper)
      1. Apologizing. 2. Interpersonal Relations. I. Title.

BF575.A75 E54 2001
158.2—dc21   2001024706

Printed in the United States of America

10 9 8 7 6 5 4 3 2 1

I dedicate this book to those who
have had the courage to apologize and
to those who were able to accept a
meaningful apology when given.

Contents

Acknowledgments

First and foremost, I wish to thank my fabulous agent, Stedman Mays, for his continued support and enthusiasm with my projects.

Next, I'd like to thank Tom Miller, my editor at John Wiley and Sons, who liked the idea for the book right away. I appreciate your input and your support throughout the editing process.

I am deeply grateful to the people I interviewed and to those friends and clients who agreed to share their stories in the hope of helping others.

I also wish to thank all those who took the time to fill out my questionnaire and those who gave permission for me to use their stories. Your feedback and stories added immensely to the book.

I wish to acknowledge the people in my life who have been gracious enough to forgive me for my past and sometimes current behavior, especially my friends: Sharon, Deborah, Patti, and Joy.

Last but certainly not least, I'd like to thank all the people at John Wiley and Sons who worked so hard on this book. A special thank-you to Lisa M. Vaia, associate managing editor, and Wendy Mount for her wonderful cover design.

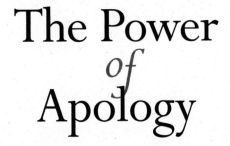

The Power
of
Apology

Introduction

My personal interest in apology began when my mother apologized for her emotionally abusive treatment toward me when I was a child. This experience was so profound and life-changing that I began to look more closely at the subject of apology. When I did, I was amazed at its healing powers. I decided it was important to share not only my own story but those of others.

My professional interest in apology began with my work with adult survivors of childhood abuse and their families. For many years, I witnessed the pain and confusion survivors felt as they struggled with forgiveness. Although many were deeply spiritual people who believed in forgiveness, they found they were unable to forgive parents and other family members for refusing to apologize or even acknowledge their wrongdoing. Even though I realized forgiveness could be very healing, I also recognized that it was extremely difficult when one has not received a meaningful apology. Therefore, unlike many professionals, I did not push forgiveness upon my clients.

In writing *The Power of Apology*, I wanted to validate those who have refused to forgive until they receive an apology. I wanted to let them know that in spite of the fact that it has now become politically correct to forgive, not forgiving when an apology is not forthcoming can be a healthy choice. And I wanted to offer alternatives such as asking for an apology.

I also wrote *The Power of Apology* for all the following reasons:

1. I want to help other adult children who are estranged from their parents to experience the healing that my mother and I experienced together.

2. I want to help others like my mother who have a difficult time apologizing to finally break through their resistance and work past their pride so that they can experience the miracle of apology for themselves and the ones they love.

3. I want to help others like myself who receive an apology to be able to accept it, embrace it, and allow it to heal them.

4. I want to show how our inability to apologize is the source of a great deal of the dysfunction in all our lives.

5. I want to show how necessary apology is to our emotional as well as physical health and well-being.

6. I want to show how important apology is to the process of forgiveness.

7. I want to show how apology has the power to transform individuals, families, groups, and communities.

Although books on forgiveness abound, there are no comprehensive books on apology. As more people recognize the importance of spirituality in their lives they are focusing on forgiveness. Apology is an important yet neglected aspect of forgiveness.

It is important to note, however, that *The Power of Apology* is *not* another book about forgiveness. The focus is on *apology*—the myriad of problems that stem from our inability to ask for and give apologies and the benefits of apologizing, of which forgiveness is only one.

Although there haven't been any books specifically devoted to apology, people are very interested in the subject. Deborah Tannen, the author of the popular book, *You Just Don't Understand*, recognized the importance of apology enough to include it in her latest book, *The Argument Culture: Moving from Debate to Dialogue*, and she and other professionals have written numerous magazine articles on the subject. But no one has put all the issues together in one book. I felt it was important to provide readers with a sourcebook for all their questions and issues with apology, whether they wanted help in:

- Overcoming their resistance to apologizing
- Learning to stop overapologizing or apologizing automatically, even when they have nothing to apologize for

- Understanding a partner or family member who refuses to apologize
- Finding a way to make amends to those with whom they have lost contact
- Teaching their children how to take responsibility for their actions
- Learning how to accept an apology

As the words *responsibility* and *forgiveness* are bandied about, many people feel frustrated. They feel pressured to take responsibility and to forgive, but they don't know how. *The Power of Apology* offers information and strategies that will help them take concrete action toward these goals.

We currently seem to be operating from two extremes when it comes to apology in North America. On the one hand, we view apology as the panacea for all that ails us. It doesn't matter how inconsiderate, selfish, or cruel we have acted; all we have to do is apologize and we are supposed to be forgiven. On the other hand, we tend to blame others and find excuses to get out of taking responsibility for our behavior. It seems to be getting harder and harder for people to acknowledge their wrongdoing and make a meaningful apology to those they have hurt or harmed.

The Power of Apology is vitally needed at a time when two conflicting messages concerning responsibility and forgiveness are being communicated to the public:

1. If anything goes wrong, don't accept responsibility for your part in it. Deny, deny, deny—and protect yourself by blaming the other person.

2. When someone does something to hurt you or your family, forgive him or her, no matter how horrific the crime or how deep the loss.

The concepts of apology and forgiveness are being misused and bastardized to the point that these life-changing gestures are at risk of becoming clichés. And our current inability to apologize has expanded into an epidemic affecting our intimate relationships, our families, our children, our business relationships, our schools, our legal system, our communities, and even our culture. My hope is that *The Power of Apology* will be the voice of clarity on the issues of responsibility and forgiveness, and will revolutionize the very notion of apology.

Apology Has the Power to Transform the World

As we witnessed with books such as *Random Acts of Kindness* and books on the importance of gratitude, sometimes the most simple concepts are the most profound. Apology, like kindness and gratitude, is profoundly powerful. It has the potential to transform the world.

There is an important connection between our inability to accept responsibility for our actions, our tendency to blame others, our high divorce rate, and the fact that our children no longer respect themselves or others. All these problems reflect the fact that we have stopped acknowledging when our actions or inaction have harmed others, that we no longer teach our children to apologize, and that instead of asking for an apology we prefer to hold grudges and distance ourselves. If we are going to heal our relationships, our children, and our world, we need to make apology an integral part of life on a daily basis. In this book I'll show how to go about doing this by offering specific, workable strategies you can use in your everyday life—at home, school, and work.

Other major issues addressed are coping with our own anger and the anger of others, how to determine whether to forgive, how to develop empathy and compassion for others, and how to take responsibility for our actions.

For example, because of the recent deluge of violence in this country, many are concerned about how to help those who feel enraged and alienated from others. Although *The Power of Apology* certainly can't solve the problems of those who have long-term depression or psychosis, it does offer strategies that can minimize feelings of alienation, anger, and resentment.

How the Book Is Organized

Focusing on the importance of apology is a simple concept, but it is revolutionary in its simplicity. The subject apology encompasses not only the issue of forgiveness but also anger management, empathy training, and the relationship between shame and pride.

The Power of Apology focuses on the importance of apology in three respects: *giving* an apology, *receiving* an apology, and *asking for* an apology. The book is based on certain life principles. At the beginning of each chapter, I present one of these principles to provide both a starting point and a focus. There are many exercises throughout the book. At the end of most chapters, I offer a series of writing exercises specifically designed to help readers process the issues addressed in the chapter and to work past any resistance they might have.

This is a very personal book for me. I share many of my own stories concerning apology and how it has transformed my life. In addition to telling my own story, I also share stories of other people whose lives have been changed by apology, including couples whose relationships were turned around by apology, parents who were able to mend their relationships with their children through apology, co-workers who improved their relationships by apologizing, victims of crime who were healed by the apology of their offender, and offenders who were healed by their act of apology to the people they victimized.

Who Will Benefit the Most from the Book

Although this book will no doubt help most people, there are some who will benefit more than others:

- Those who are interested in self-improvement will realize that apology has the potential to change their lives, just as practicing gratitude and simplicity has done for so many.

- Couples who are dedicated to maintaining a healthy and lasting relationship will benefit greatly from the strategies for getting past resentments. Many couples seek marital counseling because of the apology issue, and even those who don't often discover that a primary reason for the distance or hostility within the relationship comes from a need to apologize and be apologized to.

- Those in 12-step programs will welcome the added help they will receive as they prepare to make amends.

- Victims of emotional, physical, or sexual abuse and victims of crime will learn how to ask for an apology in such a way as to maximize their chances of receiving one. They will also learn when to work past their resistance to forgiveness and when to honor it.

- Many adult children who are estranged from their parents due to child abuse, alcoholism, or drug abuse (especially baby boomers) are now more willing to reconcile with them, but they need help in doing this.

- Parents who would like to reconcile with their adult children will benefit from my suggestions on how to apologize and how to forgive.

- Parents who want to raise children to be responsible, compassionate, and empathetic will welcome suggestions that teach and model these important values. Recent school tragedies have made us keenly aware that parents have become disconnected from their children, that influences outside the home have become far more powerful in determining behavior than we ever imagined, and that parents need to listen to their children. Parents are given tools in this book to help them gain access to their children's thoughts and feelings, and to teach their children important values not only with words but by example. Parents and children are encouraged to not only listen to one another but to respect one another's rights and feelings.

- Baby boomers beginning to move into their golden years are starting to evaluate their lives and to analyze unfinished business. Apologizing for past actions is an important aspect of this process.

- Those who are terminally ill or coming to the end of their life will benefit from the suggestions on how to do a life review and how to make amends to those they've hurt.

- Those who have deeply hurt or disappointed others, including those who have experienced a "fall from grace," need to discover that a sincere apology not only helps them to salvage their reputations and mend relationships but to forgive themselves.

- Anyone who is a group leader or in a supervisory position, including personnel managers and supervisors in business environments, school administrators, and counselors, will welcome the tools I offer for resolving work- and school-related conflicts.

- Proponents of restorative justice will welcome this book as a valuable resource for offenders and their families as well as victims and their families.

- Those dedicated to making a difference in the world will discover ways to have a positive impact. Making apology an integral part of our life can literally change the world, one person at a time.

PART ONE

The Power
of Apology

CHAPTER 1

Apology Is for Everyone

Apology is a lovely perfume; it can transform the clumsiest moment into a gracious gift.

MARGARET LEE RUNBECK

A clear conscience is more valuable than wealth.

FILIPINO PROVERB

THE POWER OF APOLOGY PRINCIPLE 1

Apology, or the lack thereof, affects literally every single person on a daily basis.

Apology changed my life. I believe it can change yours as well. Whether you have a difficult time apologizing to others when you have wronged them, difficulty receiving or accepting the apologies others have given you, or difficulty asking for the apologies that you feel are owed you, *The Power of Apology* will help you understand the obstacles that stand in your way and will offer you strategies to help work past them. It will also help you if you tend to overapologize or if you apologize automatically or too often, even if you haven't done anything wrong. Whether by force of habit, as a way to avoid conflicts, or as a symptom of low self-esteem, overapologizing can be just as troublesome as not apologizing often enough. It can affect how others perceive you, your image of yourself, and your status in a relationship or in your career.

Don't underestimate the power apology has to affect and change your life. Even if you feel you have no issues with apology, I guarantee that you will change your mind after reading this book.

But this book is about more than apology. *The Power of Apology* will teach you how to become a more humble, tolerant, compassionate, and empathetic human being. It will teach you to be less judgmental and critical of yourself and others. It will encourage you to focus on learning your own life lessons instead of thinking you can teach others their lessons. It will teach you how to conduct a life review and how to go about making amends to those you have harmed in the past. And it will help you with your issues with forgiveness, including when it is best to forgive and when it is best not to forgive.

The Power of Apology is about bringing families and friends back together when they have been estranged, as well as bringing couples and families closer together on a daily basis. It is about teaching our children to take responsibility for their actions and to have empathy and compassion for others. Ultimately, it is about saving your soul and the souls of those you love.

The Healing Power of Apology

Apology has the power to heal individuals, couples, and families. Almost like magic, apology can mend our relationships, soothe our wounds and hurt pride, and heal our broken heart.

When we apologize to someone we have hurt, disappointed, neglected, or betrayed, we give them a wonderful gift that is far more healing than almost anything else we can give. By apologizing we let the other person know that we regret having hurt him or her. Just as important, we let this person know we respect him and we care about his feelings. It becomes one of the most effective tools for mending a relationship.

Apology is not just something we do to be polite. It is an important social ritual, a way of showing respect and empathy for the wronged person. It is also a way of acknowledging an act that can't go unnoticed without compromising the relationship. Apology has the ability to disarm the anger of others, to prevent further misunderstandings, and to bridge the distances between people.

But apology has more than the power to soothe wounds or mend relationships. In some instances, it even has the ability to rehabilitate an individual, resolve conflicts, and restore social harmony. While an apology cannot truly undo harmful effects of past actions, paradoxically, if done sincerely and effectively, this is in fact what apology manages to do. When an apology is received as the gift that it is and reciprocated by the gift of forgiveness, it is nothing short of a miracle.

Apology is also an important factor in creating and maintaining healthy relationships. When we apologize to those we've hurt, slighted, disappointed, betrayed, or angered, the caring and respect we convey through our apology fosters love and trust.

When someone does something that hurts our feelings but does not apologize for it, we become resentful of that person. This resentment can take the form of our distancing ourselves from her, expressing our anger in numerous direct or indirect ways, or feeling less motivated to be considerate or caring toward her.

When your own behavior is offensive, inconsiderate, or hurtful, the recipient of your behavior grows wary of you. Whether he realizes it consciously, he feels he must be on guard. He no longer feels as relaxed around you and may even feel that he can no longer trust you. If an apology is not forthcoming, this wariness and distrust will grow. It's one thing to hurt another person, but it's another thing entirely to either not be aware that you have hurt him or to not care. If this occurs at the beginning of a relationship, it may influence whether the relationship continues. If the relationship is already an established one, it may add to a growing sense of alienation and resentment.

Apologizing to another person is one of the healthiest, most positive actions we can ever take—for ourselves, the other person, and the relationship. Apology is crucial to our mental and physical health and well-being. Research shows that receiving an apology has an obvious and positive effect on the body.

The act of apology is not only beneficial to the person receiving it but to the one giving it as well. The debilitating effects of the remorse and shame we can feel when we've hurt another person can eat away at us until we become emotionally and physically ill. By apologizing and taking responsibility for our actions, we help rid ourselves of esteem-robbing shame and guilt.

The Exchange of Shame and Power

According to psychiatrist Aaron Lazare, in an article in *Psychology Today*, what makes an apology work is the exchange of shame and power between the wrongdoer and the person who has been wronged. By apologizing, you take the shame of your offense and redirect it to yourself. You admit to hurting or diminishing someone, and, in effect, say that you are really the one who is diminished—that is, "I'm the one who was wrong, mistaken, insensitive, or stupid." In acknowledging your shame, you give the person who has been wronged the power to forgive. The exchange is at the heart of the healing process.

Apology has the power to humble the most arrogant of people. When we are able to develop the courage to admit when we are wrong and to work past our fears and resistance to apologizing, we develop a deep sense of self-respect. This self-respect can, in turn, affect our self-esteem, our self-confidence, and our overall outlook on life. When I apologize to you, I show you that I respect you and care about your feelings. I let you know that I did not intend to hurt you and that it is my intention to treat you fairly in the future. By accepting my apology, you not only show me (and yourself) that you have a generous spirit but that you are giving me and our relationship another chance. In addition, you are reminded of your own mistakes, which can encourage you to treat me and others with more respect and consideration.

Apology has the power to make all our relationships, whether personal or business, far more respectful, caring, and compassionate. If done correctly, an apology can heal humiliation and foster reconciliation and forgiveness. A genuine apology given and then accepted is one of the most profound interactions between civilized people.

My Story

When I was 35 years old, I divorced my mother. I felt that it was the only thing I could do. Not only had my mother severely damaged me with her emotional abuse as I was growing up, but she continued to emotionally abuse me every time I saw or spoke to her. I became so emotionally and physically stressed when I was with her that my health was affected. And so I made the difficult yet necessary decision to stop seeing her.

This estrangement went on for 3 years. During this time I wrote a book entitled *Divorcing a Parent*, in which I told my story about divorcing my mother and encouraged others in similar situations to consider doing the same. Then one day the phone rang, and when I picked it up the person on the other end of the line said, "I'm sorry." I recognized the voice. It was my mother.

Waves of relief washed over me. Resentment, pain, fear, and anger drained out of me. Much to my surprise, those two simple words seemed to wipe away years of pain and anger. They were the words I had been waiting to hear most of my life.

I knew that it had taken all the courage my extremely proud mother could muster to say those two words and so I didn't belabor the point at the time. The important thing was that she was saying she was sorry—something she'd never done before. I could tell by the tone of her voice that she truly regretted the way she had treated me and that she was deeply sorry.

Of course, that was only the beginning of the story. Although I believed her apology, I didn't yet know that her behavior toward me was going to be different. This I tested out slowly and carefully over several visits. But I soon realized that a miracle had occurred. My mother was a changed woman.

The years we were apart had caused her to do some serious thinking about herself and her behavior, yet this was only part of the answer. My mother had also stumbled onto another book I had written during our time apart, *The Emotionally Abused Woman*, at her local bookstore. In it I describe in detail the different types of emotionally abusive behavior, and she had recognized that she had been abusive to me.

It had taken a lot for my mother to get to the place where she could say "I'm sorry." I had to completely sever my relationship with her. It had taken years of soul-searching on her part. Finally, it had taken a miracle. I hadn't told my mother about *The Emotionally Abused Woman*. She seldom went into bookstores, and when she did she always went to the mystery section. The self-help or recovery sections would be the last places she'd ever go under normal circumstances. Even after recognizing her own behavior, it took all the courage she could muster to put aside her pride long enough to apologize.

My mother lived only 3 more years. But because she was able to apologize and because I was able to accept her apology, we were closer in those 3 years than we had ever been, and our time together was extremely healing for both of us.

Apology Is for Everyone

The Power of Apology is not just for adult children and their parents, those who have been deeply harmed by someone, or those who owe an apology for past deeds. It is for everyone. *Apology, or the lack thereof, affects literally every single person on a daily basis.*

Everyone has issues with apology to some degree or another. Some people focus on the apologies owed them—harboring their anger or lamenting about how things would be different if an apology were given. Others focus on the apologies they need to make, feeling angry or disgusted with themselves because they can't seem to find the wherewithall to apologize, or feeling hopeless because they no longer have contact with those they've hurt. And while many have difficulties apologizing, many others, particularly women, tend to take responsibility and to apologize too often.

If you have difficulties apologizing, this book will help you understand why making an apology is hard for you, will help you get past your resistance, and will teach you the most effective way to apologize. For those who have attempted apologizing in the past but have not been able to do so successfully, I will teach you how to make *meaningful* apologies—apologies that will be heard and believed. For those who yearn to restore a shattered relationship, I will answer such questions as (1) What do I have to do to show how sorry I am? (2) What will it take to bring us back together? (3) How can I take a person back into my life who has betrayed me?

If the people who have hurt or harmed you have not apologized, causing you to harbor anger and resentment and getting in the way of your being able to forgive, this book will help you in two ways: (1) It will show you ways to elicit apologies that might not otherwise be forthcoming. (2) It will help you to forgive even if you never receive an apology.

Giving, Receiving, and Asking for Apologies

For many people, receiving and accepting an apology is more difficult than giving one. This is particularly true for many women. Instead of graciously accepting apologies, women often push them away by minimizing the offense or by taking some or most of the responsibility for the offense themselves. Think of how many times you've heard a woman (or done so yourself) insist that something was merely a misunderstanding instead of allowing the other person to take full responsibility for a transgression. Accepting an apology, even when it is sincere and heartfelt, can also be difficult if you are blinded by rage or licking your wounds from the last altercation.

Learning how to ask for an apology can be as important as learning how to give one. Many of us simply distance ourselves from those who fail to apologize to us. We write the person off or feel that it is no longer safe to be vulnerable with him or her. But by asking for an apology, we can begin to bridge the gap that has grown between us. We let the other person know that we were hurt and we give him or her another chance.

By learning how to *give, receive, accept,* and *ask for* meaningful apologies, your life and your relationships will be transformed. Instead of adamantly denying wrongdoing and alienating those around you, you will be better able to admit when you are wrong and garner the respect of others. Instead of pushing away well-intentioned apologies or making excuses for wrongdoers, you'll be able to take apologies in and receive the healing that can come from them. And instead of silently seething with anger when someone hurts you, you'll be able to tell the wrongdoer why you were hurt and will be far more likely to receive the apology you deserve.

Apology and the Forgiveness Craze

Apology is an important element that seems to be missing in the current forgiveness craze. Forgiveness has become the cure-all for our problems. Many daytime talk shows have changed from anger fests to forgiveness fests as parents are reunited with their estranged children, as spouses are forgiven for their betrayal, and as politicians or leaders stand up and ask for forgiveness. We are told that forgiveness alleviates depression, enhances self-esteem, and erases past pain. Failure to forgive, we are warned, can doom us to be a victim for the rest of our life.

I was shocked to see just how far some people will go in their efforts to push forgiveness onto others when shortly after the Littleton, Colorado, shootings a reporter stuck a microphone in the face of a grieving parent and asked, "Have you forgiven your child's murderers?" I was even more shocked when I heard the parent say, "Yes." Forgiveness is far more difficult and complex than most people understand. It is a process that takes time and dedication. Most importantly, the giving and receiving of *meaningful* apologies is often required before true forgiveness can occur. It is painfully difficult, if not impossible, for those who have been hurt to forgive if a meaningful apology is not forthcoming. And it is equally difficult to forgive yourself when you don't have the strength to apologize to those you've hurt.

The Need for an Apology in Order to Forgive

There is no doubt that we should be able to forgive. But we can't always do so. Many people are unable to forgive, no matter how hard they try. Apology is the missing key.

Think of an incident when you felt wronged by another person. What did you want from that person in order to forgive him or her? Most people say they want an apology. But why is this the case? It isn't just the words *I'm sorry* that we need to hear. We need the wrongdoer to take responsibility for his or her actions and we need to know that the wrongdoer feels regret or remorse for having harmed us. This expression of responsibility and remorse helps us to gain compassion and empathy for the offender—which are both necessary if we are going to be able to forgive.

The Exercises

Throughout the book I offer information and personal stories (my own and those of clients and friends) that will help you come to a deeper understanding of the importance of apology and encourage you to make apology an integral part of your life. In addition, I offer exercises that will help you resolve your issues with apology, whether you have difficulty apologizing, accepting apologies, or asking for apologies. Please don't underestimate the importance of these exercises. While it may be a natural urge to want to skip the exercises in your enthusiasm to move forward in the book, you'll gain much more from the book if you take the time to complete each one.

Since I can't work with each one of you in person, my exercises are the next best thing to working with me in therapy. And it has been my experience that those who pause to complete the exercises in my books experience many more profound changes in their life than those who do not.

EXERCISE
Your Apology Lists

This first writing exercise will help you begin the process of discovering your issues with apology.

A. Make a list of all the people to whom you feel you owe an apology. Write down whoever comes to mind. Don't worry about whether your list is complete (we'll work on helping you make a more complete list later in the book).

   1. Write about what you noticed or learned from making this list. For example:

- Do you have a lot of people to apologize to or a few?
- Do you have difficulty thinking about apologizing?
- Does your pride get in the way?
- Did you notice yourself feeling stubborn and a need to be right?
- Were you too busy thinking about what the other person did to you to think about apologizing to him or her?

   2. Write about who you feel most inclined to apologize to and why. For example, does it seem easier to apologize to those to whom you are closest (such as your partner, your family, or your close friends) or to those to whom you are more distant (such as business associates or acquaintances)?

   3. To whom do you feel most resistant to making an apology? Write about why you think this is the case.

B. Now make a list of all the people who you feel owe you an apology.

   1. Write about what you noticed or learned from making this list. For example:

- Are there a lot of people who owe you an apology?
- Does it make you uncomfortable thinking about asking these people for an apology?

- Do you think you have the courage to ask for the apologies you feel are owed you?
- Why have you not asked for an apology for these offenses before now?

2. Write about who you feel most inclined to ask for an apology and why. For example, does it seem easier to ask those to whom you are closest or those to whom you are more distant?

3. To whom do you feel most resistant to asking for an apology? Write about why you think this is the case.

⚮

We all have plenty to apologize for. Every single day we do things that hurt other people's feelings or that show disrespect. We're impatient and rude to store clerks; we snap at our co-workers; we become defensive and argue unnecessarily with our friends; we say hurtful things to our partner in the heat of an argument; we misjudge a friend's intentions when he or she tries to help us; we falsely accuse our children of lying.

Even when we are aware that we have hurt another's feelings and feel a twinge of remorse, most of us let these moments pass without apologizing. We tell ourselves that it isn't all that important—they'll get over it. We rationalize that the other person has done the same thing to us. We may even tell ourselves that we'll apologize later but then forget to do so.

Unfortunately, apology has gone the way of many other social gestures that convey respect and consideration for others (such as "please" and "excuse me"). One of the many goals of this book is to help bring back this gesture of respect and caring, perhaps encouraging everyone once again to begin saying other important words as well.

The following list contains some of the most significant changes *The Power of Apology* can inspire:

- It will make it easier for those who need to make apologies and amends to others to do so, thus helping to relieve the shame and guilt they have harbored. Shame and guilt can destroy self-esteem, causing hopelessness and a lack of desire to become a better person.

- It will not only make it easier for people to apologize to one another but to ask for an apology when they feel they are owed one instead of lashing out at the other person or harboring unexpressed anger.

- It will help cut down on the increasing divorce rate by offering a unique tool to help couples communicate their anger and frustration and move on to forgiveness.

- It will provide parents a unique way to teach their children responsibility, compassion, empathy, and humility, as well as to show them that they do not have to be perfect.

- It will bring families back together and help heal the distance that time, pain, and resentment have created.

- It will offer families a way to air their differences, find a common ground, and heal the pain of everyday hurts.

- It will help provide closure for those in midlife, those who are ill, and those who are preparing for death.

- It will help readers to complete their unfinished business and heal the wounds of childhood.

- It offers those parents who have passed on the legacy of child abuse a way to acknowledge this to their children, to apologize to them, and to begin to break the cycle of abuse.

- It will help those who have "fallen from grace" to apologize for their misdeeds, to forgive themselves, and to become a better person.

- It offers an alternative to our current tendency to blame and shame wrongdoers by offering a way to teach empathy, encourage remorse, and provide a plan for restitution.

CHAPTER 2

Why Learning to Give, Receive, and Ask for Apologies Is So Important

Confess your sins to one another.

NEW TESTAMENT, BOOK OF JAMES

Words are a form of action, capable of influencing change.

INGRID BENGIS

THE POWER OF APOLOGY PRINCIPLE 2
Apology reminds us that each person (including ourselves) deserves to be respected and treated fairly.

We commonly say that we *owe* someone an apology or that we need to *give* an apology. We also say we *received* an apology or we *accept* an apology. These words might imply that something tangible is being exchanged. Yet contrary to the logic of our economic marketplace or our conceptions of social exchange, the apology itself is the only compensation. In our money-driven, consumer-oriented world, there can be no more testament to the power of apology than this. It boggles the mind to understand how the expression of regret itself serves as reparation without requiring additional actions on the part of the wrongdoer, but this is exactly what apology accomplishes.

The Importance of Apology to Social Order

In the dark days of our history, if someone offended another person there was no such thing as an apology. Instead, the offending person would be challenged to a duel. As we became more civilized, we decided that although our honor and our reputation were certainly important, they were not so important that we should defend them with our life. (It is interesting to note that in today's gang culture, there seems to be a return to the old duel mentality—albeit with guns instead of swords.)

We came to understand that we needed a way to protect our honor without bloodshed. And we needed a formal way to rehabilitate ourselves when we offended someone. This is how apology was born. (For more information on the history of apology, refer to *Mea Culpa: The Sociology of Apology and Reconciliation* by Nicholas Tavuchis.)

Apology recognizes the community's need for individuals to adhere to certain agreed-upon rules. When someone breaks a rule of society, even if it is a mere infraction of etiquette, there is an expectation that the person apologize for the offense. This not only shows respect for those who may have been offended by the infraction but in essence also shows respect for the rule that was broken.

Apology fosters compassion and forgiveness. While society could not run properly without established rules of behavior, we all know that humans are not perfect. Therefore, even though there is an expectation that the majority of people will follow the rules most of the time, room has been made for the likelihood that some people will sometimes break the rules. When this occurs, we offer the individual a way to reenter society with honor—the apology. By admitting their offense and formally apologizing, individuals essentially promise to once again abide by the rules of society.

The Importance of Apology in Religious and Spiritual Institutions

Apology has always been intrinsically linked with forgiveness and for this reason it has been a mainstay in most religions. For example, the act of confession within the Catholic Church is essentially an apology to God. It has all the important components of apology: a statement of regret, an acceptance of responsibility for one's actions, a promise not to repeat the offense, and the request for forgiveness.

While other religions may not have as formal or as accessible a way for their congregants to confess, most encourage apology in the form of some kind of confession. In the Jewish tradition it has long been the custom to seek forgiveness from family members, friends, neighbors, and colleagues during the time of the High Holy Days. For example, it is not uncommon in the synagogues of Eastern Europe to see people turn to fellow congregants and friends and quietly ask for forgiveness.

In addition to religious institutions, there are other institutions—just as powerful and just as spiritual as most formal religions—that have made apology an integral part of their basic tenets. The 12-step programs such as AA (Alcoholics Anonymous), NA (Narcotics Anonymous), GA (Gamblers Anonymous), SAA (Sex Addicts Anonymous), and OA (Overeaters Anonymous) all advocate apology as a powerful tool to be used in recovery.

Most people who have an addiction to anything—whether it is alcohol, drugs, gambling, sex, or food—discover during the recovery process that their way of dealing with other people is defective and that they harbor a great deal of guilt and shame concerning their treatment of others. They learn that if they are to gain and maintain abstinence and find serenity—two of the main goals of recovery from any compulsion or addiction—they have to acquire better ways of dealing with other people—ways that bring them joy instead of pain.

Step 8 of the 12-step program is designed to help those in recovery examine their relationships (both past and present) in order to discover the patterns of behavior that have done harm to others and themselves. This is accomplished by making a written list of all persons they have harmed and by working toward a willingness to make amends to each person on their list.

In step 9 of 12-step programs, people are encouraged to make direct amends to those they have harmed, except when doing so would injure themselves or others. This involves acknowledging their faults and then taking direct action to remedy the damage they did or to repay the losses they caused. Most who complete step 9 feel freed from their past mistakes in a miraculous way. Their lives are immeasurably changed, their broken relationships are mended, and the ill will that for years poisoned their hearts is washed away.

Although making amends is more than just saying "I'm sorry," apologizing for past actions is a major part of step 9.

Apology and the Law

In the distant past, particularly in ancient tribal societies, if a person took responsibility and apologized for his actions, his victims and the community were often far less inclined to punish him. This is still the case with tribal nations such as that of the Maori in New Zealand, who focus far more on apology and on the creation of a plan of restitution that satisfies all those concerned than on punishing wrongdoers.

Although our civil and criminal justice systems are quite different today, focusing far more on punishment than on righting the wrong, many people have been willing to drop lawsuits or criminal charges if the person who harmed them apologized. And receiving an apology is so important to some people that they are willing to forget and/or forgive the most heinous of crimes if the offender shows remorse and apologizes. For many, having someone accept responsibility for a wrongdoing and express remorse for the harm he or she caused is far more healing than any punishment the wrongdoer would ever be forced to experience.

When Barbara and Lyle returned home from dinner with their 4-year-old daughter, Cameron, a few years ago, they were shocked and frightened by what they saw. Their house was in shambles. Books and clothes had been tossed on the floor, and the contents of drawers lay in piles everywhere. Some of Barbara's jewelry was missing, as was their CD player.

For weeks afterward, Barbara remained very upset and frightened. "I was angry because my daughter was traumatized by the situation, and it was upsetting to all of us to walk into our house and find that someone had gone through all our things. It felt like such an invasion of our privacy. I lived in constant fear that the person would come back and this time maybe he would harm us."

Fortunately, the family lived in a small town. It didn't take long before police were able to track down their thief—15-year-old Randy. They were even able to return Barbara's jewelry and the CD player.

"I was so relieved. Now I didn't have to worry about some

unknown crazy man out there who could return at any time," Barbara said.

Since this was Randy's first offense and he seemed genuinely sorry for what he'd done, he qualified for a new program called Restorative Justice in which victims and offenders had the opportunity to meet face-to-face. Lyle was reluctant. He felt too angry at the boy to face him. "Frankly, I was afraid of what I'd say or do."

But Barbara insisted: "I wanted to confront this boy and tell him how much he upset our family. I wanted him to know what he had done to us."

And so the meeting was set up. In turn, both Barbara and Lyle told Randy how the break-in had affected them. Randy had to listen without interrupting. Then it was Randy's turn. He told Barbara and Lyle how very sorry he was. He told them he hadn't intended to frighten them—that he hadn't thought about how the residents of the house might feel. He said he had learned his lesson and would never do it again.

Lyle's anger subsided once he heard Randy's apology. "I believed he was genuinely sorry, and this made me see him as a mixed-up kid instead of as a monster."

Barbara was surprised at how she now felt toward Randy. "I actually felt sorry for him. We learned from the authorities that his father had left home when he was only six and that his mother worked nights in order to make a living. It was clear that this boy was in trouble. This was the first time he'd broken the law."

Part of the restorative justice process is for the victims to make recommendations as to what the offender's punishment would be. As Barbara explained, "I didn't really need for Randy to be punished. His remorse and his apology were enough for me. But I felt we had a chance to help turn him around, so in lieu of jail time we decided that Randy's punishment would be for him to clean our house once a week for three months. He'd made such a mess of everything in our house—it seemed like an appropriate punishment."

But the connection between Randy and this family didn't end once the 3 months were up. The family has become very involved in Randy's life. Lyle has become a surrogate father to Randy, taking him to ball games and on fishing trips. Randy comes over almost every night to do his homework when his mother is working. As far as Barbara and Lyle are concerned, he's just another member of the family.

Unfortunately, in these litigious times, when people are being sued right and left, there isn't much encouragement for apologizing and taking responsibility for our actions. If you are in a car accident and you know you caused it, your natural inclination is to say "I'm sorry," but you probably won't. You've learned to hold your tongue from lawyers and insurance companies, who admonish "Never admit fault."

But the need for victims to receive an apology is so strong that it has even begun to change our laws. Recently, the law has recognized the importance of apology to such an extent that in Massachusetts a bill was passed to make it safe to say "I'm sorry." The bill stipulates that saying "I'm sorry" does not make a person legally liable. (The bill specifically stipulates that protection is afforded only to those who say "I'm sorry," not to the words "It was my fault.") A similar bill is also being considered in California.

Apology and Our Interpersonal Relationships

The most important application of apology is on the personal level. Many people have become estranged from family members and close friends because the wrongdoer refused to apologize. Long-term friendships have been broken, families have been split apart, and marriages have been seriously tested or even ended over the issue of apology.

In contrast, long-estranged friends and family members have been brought back together by a simple apology, and marriages have been saved when one partner apologizes to another. One simple apology can melt even the hardest of hearts and tear down the strongest of walls.

Apology recognizes and honors an individual's need to protect herself when she has been hurt. In essence, by recognizing the need to apologize, we are stating to the individual we have harmed: *I recognize I have hurt you and that you must shut me out and put up walls to protect yourself from me. Therefore, I will humble myself before you by apologizing to you, temporarily giving you my power in order to show I am no longer a threat. I also understand that you are leery of me, that you no longer trust me, and that I must now win back your trust. By admitting my offense, I begin to earn that trust back.*

Reasons to Apologize

As part of my research for this book, I conducted an informal poll with an apology questionnaire. One of the questions I asked was to list the top three behaviors that most warrant an apology. Based on the results of my questionnaire, the major reasons for apologizing are as follows (these results were consistent with my experience with clients):

- Rude or inconsiderate treatment
- Lying/deceit
- Put-downs or sarcasm
- Thoughtlessness
- Breaking a confidence
- Impatience
- Negative attitude
- Disrespect
- Negative judgment or misjudgment
- Breaking a promise
- Gossiping, backbiting, spreading lies
- Unfairness
- Subjecting someone to emotional, physical, or sexual abuse
- Meanness or cruelty
- Being late or forgetting a meeting or appointment

EXERCISE
Discovering Your Top Three

A. Make your own list of the top three offenses committed by others that you feel warrant an apology.

B. List three reasons why you believe other people do not apologize.

C. List the three offenses you are most guilty of that you feel warrant an apology.

D. Make a list of the three major reasons why you have difficulty apologizing.

Why Giving Apologies Is So Important

As much as we all want and need apologies, it is equally important
to us to apologize for our errors and omissions. We all secretly long
to admit our mistakes and ask for forgiveness. Most of us have the
tendency to feel guilt or shame when we do something wrong, and
our guilt or shame eats away at us until we admit our wrongdoing
and apologize to the person or persons we have harmed. When we
apologize, we feel better because our guilt and shame have been
assuaged. If our apology is accepted, we feel forgiven and can therefore forgive ourselves much more easily.

There are five reasons why apologizing to another person is so
important:

1. Apologizing to another person shows respect.

2. Apologizing shows that you are capable of taking responsibility for your actions.

3. Apologizing shows that you care about the other person's
   feelings.

4. Apologizing shows that you are a considerate person who is
   capable of empathizing with other people.

5. By apologizing to another person, you *disarm* him or her.
   The other person no longer feels that you are a threat and
   your apology often quiets the person's anger.

Think of how much better you feel after you have apologized to
someone you care about. Not only do you likely feel relieved of
some of your guilt or shame, but you probably feel better about
yourself for having had the courage to admit you were wrong. You
probably feel closer to the other person, since knowing you have
wronged someone often causes you to distance yourself from that
person. Apologizing can also clarify a situation, often preventing
further misunderstandings. For example, we've all felt uncomfortable after a meeting, a date, or a phone conversation because something just didn't feel right, or there seemed to be a great deal of

tension between ourselves and the other person. We wonder whether it was something we said or if the other person was upset with us. By giving a preemptive apology, such as saying "I'm sorry if I have offended you in some way," we can often clear up a misunderstanding.

The Reasons Why Most People Apologize

There are four primary reasons why people apologize:

1. Regret from causing someone to suffer and the wish to diminish or end the other person's pain
2. To relieve oneself of a guilty conscience
3. To salvage or restore a relationship
4. To escape punishment or in order to "look good" to others

The next time you feel like apologizing, ask yourself, *Why am I doing this? What is the purpose of my apology?*

The best reason to apologize is the first. This shows that you are capable of having empathy for the other person and that you genuinely feel bad about what you did. It also shows caring, since you are willing to set aside your pride to help relieve the pain of the one you hurt.

Although the second reason is less magnanimous and more selfish than the first, at least it shows that you are capable of feeling remorse for your actions and that you do in fact have a conscience. While the third reason can be less honorable than the first and second, it shows that you care enough for the person you offended or hurt that you would like to remove the obstacles in the relationship.

The fourth reason, however, is not a good reason for apologizing. If this is your reason for wanting to apologize, it is probably best if you either don't apologize at all or postpone your apology until you gain more empathy and caring.

Why Receiving an Apology Is So Important

Apology is important to our emotional, spiritual, and even physical health. Research shows that receiving an apology actually changes the body chemistry of the person being apologized to. Blood pressure decreases, the heart rate slows down, and breathing becomes more steady. Although we don't exactly know why the body reacts in this way, we can make some assumptions.

If we are angry with someone, it makes sense that our body will be more tense, our blood pressure will be higher, and so forth. When we receive an apology and the respect that goes along with it, our anger usually subsides.

Apology also shows acknowledgment that you have indeed been harmed and have a right to feel hurt or angry. This kind of validation is incredibly healing. We all want our feelings to be acknowledged, especially when they have been hurt or we have been emotionally damaged. We want the other person to show us that he knows he has hurt us.

When a person apologizes, we no longer experience him as a personal threat. Going back to the old fight-or-flight days, a person couldn't afford to have an enemy because it meant having to constantly look over one's shoulder. When an enemy apologizes, this person is admitting he was wrong, and this takes away his power and the threat that he will continue to be our enemy.

Having those who have wronged us apologize for their actions is one of our deepest, most abiding desires. When an apology is not forthcoming, we feel cheated and unable to let go of our anger and resentment. Think of the number of times you've heard someone say "All I wanted was an apology," or "Until I receive an apology, I can't forgive."

Receiving an apology from those who have hurt us doesn't reverse the damage, but it helps tremendously. Recently a friend of mine received a letter from an old boyfriend apologizing for the way he treated her during their relationship. My friend was surprised at how much the apology affected her. Even though she hadn't heard from or seen this man in many years, his cruel words had stayed with her. In essence, by apologizing he had taken his words back along with some of the pain she still carried.

We want an apology when someone hurts us because we want to know the other person feels bad for what he or she did. Although the wrongdoer can't take back what has already been done, knowing he or she feels sorry about it makes us feel better.

For many people, to attempt to forgive without an apology is to take the risk that the other person is not sorry and does not take responsibility for her actions, and they are simply not willing to do this. There are, of course, people who can do so. Because of their belief system and/or spiritual practice, they may have reached a certain level of understanding and compassion that helps them bypass their need for an apology. These people are truly rare (the Pope forgiving the man who attempted to assassinate him is a good example). Most people need an apology before they are able to forgive. It's a very human need that we shouldn't be ashamed of.

Validating Perceptions

Apologies are important because they can validate our perceptions. If we complain to someone about his or her behavior or attitude and that person denies any wrongdoing, we may have one of two typical reactions. We may become angry at the person's denial and begin to distance ourselves from him or her, feeling that it is hopeless to try to deal with this person, or we may begin to doubt our perceptions.

Those who come from families where there was a great deal of denial (such as when one or both parents were alcoholics or when one family member was emotionally, physically, or sexually abusive to another) grow up questioning their own perceptions. When such a person encounters another's denial, he is far more likely to doubt his own perceptions than to insist he is right.

You Tried To Tell Me . . .

Some people have both reactions—anger and doubt—as was my situation when I confronted a dear friend about her tendency to be controlling. I love and respect my friend very much. We have a very deep spiritual connection and she is the only person, besides my previous therapists, who has been able to fully share my pain concerning my abusive childhood. I have been there for her in the same way.

But my dear friend had a tendency to control every situation. Her need to be in control went way beyond having to be the one to choose which restaurant or movie we would go to, although that was the case. She couldn't even allow someone else to drive. The most uncomfortable aspect of her dominating nature was that she tried to control other people. For example, she always had something to say about the way her (grown) children were living their lives, and if they didn't do as she expected, she became angry and withdrew from them.

Since my friend and I are so close and had confronted each other's behavior many times, I felt it was important to tell her about this problem, especially when she tried to control me. But the few times I brought up the issue, she denied having any such tendency. As time passed, I became more and more angry and distant. At times, I doubted my perceptions, thinking that perhaps I was wrong after all.

I discovered I just couldn't tolerate my friend's need to control me any longer and for several years we drifted apart. She remarried and became absorbed in her relationship and I was in a new relationship myself. But when my friend went through a major life crisis, my love for her overshadowed all of my past resentments and I was there to comfort her. During this time, we once again became close.

Then one day, several months after her crisis had passed, my friend and I were having a heart-to-heart talk when she said to me, "I'm sorry I've been so controlling. You tried to tell me about it years ago, but I just couldn't see it. I'm terribly sorry." Once again, I had the experience of having a heavy weight lifted off my shoulders, just as I had with my mother. All the resentment I had felt toward her vanished in an instant and I suddenly felt the distance between us dissolve. I felt closer to her than ever. I could now trust my friend instead of feeling as if I had to protect myself from her.

Something else happened when my friend apologized to me—she validated my perception. Having grown up with a crazy-making mother who would blatantly do something and then turn around and deny having done it, I had always secretly been afraid that my perceptions weren't accurate. Even when I felt certain of something, if the person denied it, I would become confused, suddenly feel dizzy, and wonder whether it was, in fact, me who had misperceived the experience. My friend's apology validated my perception of her, which was itself a wonderful gift.

As you can see, an apology is more than just saying "I'm sorry." It is also:

- A statement of recognition of the pain that was caused
- An expression of regret or remorse for what was done
- An acknowledgment of responsibility
- A peace offering—an expression of a desire for reconciliation
- A plea for understanding, compassion, and ultimately forgiveness
- A validation of the other person's perceptions

The Negative Results of Not Receiving an Apology

As much as receiving an apology benefits us, *not* receiving an apology harms us. This is true for several reasons.

We tend to stay angry with and distant from our loved ones when we feel they owe us an apology. With each day that goes by without an apology, we often feel increasingly cheated and embittered.

Not receiving an apology can cause us to remain focused on the past. For example, those who were abandoned, deceived, or betrayed by previous lovers often fantasize about the day when their ex will humbly ask for their forgiveness—the day they will finally feel vindicated. This prevents them from moving forward and from trusting and loving again. Adult children who were neglected or abused by their parents long for the day when their parents will finally come out of denial and acknowledge how their behavior damaged their children. Unfortunately, this apology seldom if ever comes, and continuing to hope for it keeps these adult children stuck in the past, full of hatred, and unable to open their hearts to others.

Estranged relatives and friends often refuse to reconcile until an apology is given. And victims of violent crime often refuse to go on with their lives until the criminals finally admit their guilt.

It has been said an apology is only powerful if we refuse to give it. While giving an apology can certainly be powerful, there is some truth to this statement. By not apologizing, we are clearly making a powerful statement to the person we've offended. And when we do not apologize for our misdeeds and slights, we tend to respect ourselves less and expect less of ourselves. Consequently, our behavior continues to deteriorate along with our relationships with others.

The Importance of Accepting an Apology

It is also important to be able to accept apologies. When we accept someone's apology, we don't just imply that we are letting bygones be bygones; we also express:

- A recognition that the other person feels regret or remorse for what he or she did

- A belief that the other person is truly sorry and will make every attempt to not repeat the behavior or action

- A willingness to understand and have compassion for the wrongdoer
- A desire for reconciliation
- A willingness to forgive

These are all powerful statements. Those whose apologies are accepted feel far less shame and guilt for their actions than those whose apologies are rejected.

Accepting an apology is in essence a vote of confidence on your part, since you are saying that you believe in the basic goodness of the other person and in his or her ability to change. This vote of confidence is empowering and esteeming for that person.

The Importance of Asking for an Apology

Not speaking up when someone treats you with disrespect, inconsideration, or cruelty is tantamount to giving that person permission to treat you poorly. Asking for an apology is a polite but assertive way of telling the other person that you expect to be treated with respect, consideration, and kindness and that you will accept nothing less.

When we ask for an apology, we not only ask the other person to say he or she is sorry but also to:

- Acknowledge the pain or inconvenience he or she caused
- Express regret or remorse for causing such pain
- Take responsibility for his or her actions
- Make restitution or express his or her intention to not repeat the act

Even if you are rebuffed, your efforts are not in vain. Your willingness to speak up and your acknowledgment of the hurt the other person caused will free you from some of your anger and pain and will begin the process of healing your wounds. You've given the person the chance to recognize her hurtful behavior, and that is a great gift. If she doesn't choose to appreciate your gift, you now have more information about her than you did before. This information may encourage you to protect yourself around her, but at least you won't be eating yourself up with anger.

EXERCISE
Your Personal Experience with Apology

A. Write about an experience you've had with apology (either giving, receiving, or asking for one) that was significant to you in some way. Include all the following issues in your narrative:

  1. Why was this experience significant to you?

  2. How did this experience affect you?

  3. Do you think that giving, receiving, or asking for this apology changed you in any way or changed the relationship? If so, how?

  4. Do you think the apology changed the other person? If so, how?

CHAPTER 3

Why Apologizing Is Difficult for Some and Too Easy for Others

To rush into explanations and excuses is always a sign of weakness.

AGATHA CHRISTIE

When there is no shame, there is no honor.

WEST AFRICAN PROVERB

THE POWER OF APOLOGY PRINCIPLE 3

There tend to be two types of people: those who have difficulty empathizing with others and those who tend to focus too much attention on the needs and feelings of others.

As the Elton John song states, *sorry* can be the hardest word to say. But why is this so? Since the need to be apologized to and the need to apologize are both so compelling, why is it so difficult for many of us to do it? And why is it that some people seem to be able to apologize much more easily than others? We'll explore these questions in this chapter.

We Have to Be Carefully Taught

Neither apology nor forgiveness are innate qualities; they must be learned and encouraged. Although it is human nature to feel some pang of sorrow or regret when we hurt someone, we also have a tendency to harden our heart in anticipation of their response. It is far too risky to remain open and vulnerable to someone who has reason to be angry with us, someone who by all rights is liable to retaliate.

By the same token, when someone hurts our feelings, betrays us, or lets us down, our natural, most human response is to defend ourselves against the hurt (and against the other person) by hardening our heart to them. This only makes sense. Why would we want to remain open and vulnerable to someone who has already hurt us and who is therefore capable of hurting us still further?

Apology offers us an honorable way to seek redemption from others and a way to forgive others their offenses without jeopardizing our honor. It makes it safe for us to be vulnerable to one another once again. But in spite of the fact that apology is one of our most powerful social skills, today little attention is paid to learning this important skill or to teaching it to our children. The sad truth is that most people don't know how to give a genuine apology. Even though our intentions may be good, we often botch our attempts at apology and make matters worse.

Many of us have been raised with the Christian belief that we should forgive others as we have been forgiven. But we haven't been taught how to do this. Nor have we been taught the important role apology plays in the act of forgiveness. But in other cultures and other religions, the importance of apology is taught and encouraged. In his wonderful book, *How to Forgive When You Can't Forget*, Rabbi Charles Klein tells the story of how, during his first year of rabbinical studies in Jerusalem, he noticed students preparing for Yom Kippur, the Jewish Day of Atonement, by placing little notes on the bulletin board, asking the forgiveness of anyone they may have hurt or offended during the past year. The messages were simple, but they created an atmosphere in which forgiveness and reconciliation were possible.

Apology and Our Cultural Conditioning

Our current difficulty with making apologies is partly due to our cultural conditioning. In her book, *The Argument Culture*, Deborah

Tannen, Ph.D., professor of linguistics at Georgetown University, wrote about what she calls our "argument culture," in which being right is far more important than accepting responsibility:

> In public discourse all around us, human relationships are modeled on a metaphorical battle between two polarized sides. Television shows and news reports frame issues in this way: . . . the underlying dynamic is like a shoot-out between two gunslingers, which one must lose while the other wins.
>
> Against the backdrop of the argument culture, the fear of losing becomes paramount. Apologizing, then, can seem all the more like a defeat.

We are discouraged from taking responsibility for our actions and apologizing for our wrongdoing because we have been raised in a culture that causes us to fear making mistakes. Those who make mistakes are seen as losers. And because of the highly competitive nature of our culture, achieving and winning are valued far more than courtesy, kindness, and a concern for the consequences of our actions. Some people even believe that apologizing is a sign of weakness, and not apologizing is a recommended strategy for staying in control.

A Sign of Weakness

Even though most of us feel better after giving or receiving an apology, there is an equally powerful opposing drive within each of us—that of protecting our ego, our pride, and our carefully constructed and defended public self. We don't apologize because to do so is to admit we are flawed and fallible.

To many, particularly men, apologizing reflects weakness. A friend recently told me of an exchange he heard at a friend's home. The husband had done something to offend his wife in front of everyone present and she jokingly said, "I think you owe me an apology." Instead of apologizing, he boldly stated, "I *never* apologize." As far as my friend was concerned, that statement said a lot about this man. It seemed as if his whole identity was invested in withholding his "I'm sorry," and he seemed to wear his refusal to apologize as a badge of honor.

Since apologizing entails admitting fault, many people see this as a sign of weakness, inviting further assault, even though the effect is usually the opposite. Not apologizing or apologizing badly is seen as a face-saving maneuver for these people.

Giving up Power

For others, apologizing means admitting they are wrong, which they translate into giving up power. My friend, Stella, recently told me, "My husband only apologizes when he knows he's wrong. Since he's so sure he's right all the time, he hardly ever apologizes."

For many men, being right bestows power. If a man wants to have the upper hand, it's essential that he be right all the time.

Of course, there are women who have an equally difficult time apologizing. As my friend, Mary, told me, "In our relationship the roles are reversed. Tony is the one who cries easily and he is really good about apologizing. I'm the one who has a problem expressing my feelings and I hardly ever apologize, even when I know I'm wrong. I only apologize if I can do it without giving anything up." When I asked her what she was afraid of giving up, she thought for a while and then said, "Power."

A Matter of Pride

To apologize is to set aside our pride long enough to admit our imperfections; for some, this feels far too vulnerable, too dangerous. Apologizing also overrides our tendency to make excuses or blame others. This acceptance of responsibility for our own actions may be so out of character that it is nearly impossible.

On a *Nightline* program shortly after the Littleton, Colorado, shootings, Ted Koppel held a town meeting with the families of the children who were killed in Jonesboro, Arkansas. Unbeknownst to anyone, it turned out that in attendance were both the husband of the murdered Jonesboro teacher and the mother of Mitchell Johnson, one of the two young killers.

When the teacher's husband, Mr. Wright, discovered that Gretchen Woodard, the mother of Mitchell Johnson, was in attendance, he complained that it had been 13 months and he still hadn't heard an apology from the parents of either boy. Very poignantly, he stated, "Don't make the victims have to ask for an apology."

When Gretchen Woodard stood up, she defended herself and told how she too had suffered, but no apology was forthcoming.

Even after Ted Koppel invited her to apologize, she said that she had already done so through the media. When he pursued the matter still further, suggesting that she never apologized face-to-face and now had the chance, she still refused.

People like Gretchen Woodard need to be encouraged to set aside their pride, to be willing to expose their vulnerability and discover that they are not diminished or destroyed in the process. They need to be reminded of how much we all desire and need to be apologized to. And many need to be taught *how* to apologize in a way that will be heard and accepted.

The Fear of Consequences

In addition to our pride being in the way, the fear of consequences can prevent us from taking responsibility for our actions and apologizing. Many people fear that if they take the risk of apologizing they may be rejected. *What if he never speaks to me again?* and *What if she leaves me?* are two of our most common fears.

Others fear that by apologizing they risk being exposed or having their reputation ruined. *What if he tells everyone what I did?* is the common fear of those who fear this consequence. Some people fear that by admitting fault they will lose the respect of others. *What if she thinks I'm incompetent? What if they think I'm getting too soft?* Still others fear retaliation. *What if he yells at me? What if she tries to get revenge?*

And as I wrote earlier, the fear of retaliation, exposure, or even arrest may prevent us from doing what we know we need to do. Even those who would like to apologize for wrongdoing hold back out of fear of being sued or arrested, or because of the advice of legal counsel.

The Lack of Awareness

Many people don't apologize because they are oblivious to the effect their actions have on others. They don't apologize because they are simply unaware that they have anything to apologize for. They may be so focused on what others have done to harm them that they can't see how they have harmed others, or they may be so self-focused that they are unable to see the effect of their behavior on others. No matter what anyone says and no matter how many people tell them they are wrong, they just don't see it.

Each person suffers in one way or another and each of us tries to end that suffering in any way we can. Sometimes, in a last-ditch effort to end our suffering, we choose to close off our mind or harden our heart. Even though we accomplish our goal of not being able to feel our pain, we also stop feeling the pain of others. When this happens, we may act in callous, selfish, or even cruel ways without knowing it. We may give the impression that we don't care when, in fact, we are just blind to the effects of our actions.

In the past, I've tended to be somewhat oblivious that my behavior hurt other people. At times, I took this to such an extreme that even when people told me I had hurt their feelings, I would minimize my behavior and discount their feelings. I would sometimes go so far as to accuse the other person of being too sensitive or of misinterpreting my actions.

But ever since my mother apologized to me and I became aware that I too had a tendency to be emotionally abusive, I have been working on myself. If someone tells me I hurt her feelings, I try to move past any defensiveness I might feel and apologize. This behavior has brought me enormous rewards. I am far more aware of my actions than I once was and now catch myself when I am being inconsiderate, self-absorbed, or critical. If someone seems to be more distant than usual or is short with me, I take a look at my behavior toward that person to see if I might have inadvertently offended her.

Some people are unaware of how much an apology benefits the person they've offended, as well as themselves. Too embarrassed to apologize, many people simply distance themselves from the person they have offended or hope that in time the offense will be forgotten. These people need to be educated about how regular apologies can greatly improve all types of relationships—whether between husband and wife, parent and child, or between co-workers—and that by not apologizing they are adding insult to injury.

The Inability to Empathize or Overempathizing

By far, the most significant reason why so many of us have difficulty apologizing is that we lack empathy for others—that quality that enables us to put ourselves in the place of the other person. In order to truly apologize, we need to be able to imagine how our behavior or attitude has affected the other person. Some of us have to be reminded how to have empathy and others have to be taught.

Generally, there tend to be two types of people: those who have difficulty empathizing with others, and those who tend to focus too much attention on the needs and feelings of others and not enough on themselves.

Some people are quick to excuse themselves when they make a mistake or do something wrong. They reason: *I'll do better next time. We all make mistakes. What's done is done—no use beating myself up for it.* Ironically, when someone hurts *them*, they feel deeply wounded and think: *How could he do this? How dare she do this to me?* They find it very difficult to forgive, to let things go, to put things in the past. They want forgiveness but are unable to forgive.

The opposite type of person tends to justify the other person's actions and to refrain from judging *because, after all, we've all done such things.* But when they are the ones who make a mistake or hurt someone else (even unintentionally), it is a completely different story. While they ooze forgiveness and understanding for other people, they can't seem to muster even a little self-forgiveness. Instead they think: *I should have known better. How could I have done such a thing?*

There is a significant difference between having empathy for someone (putting yourself in the other person's place) and rationalizing, justifying, or making excuses for the person's behavior. If you tend to blame yourself if something goes wrong, to doubt your own perceptions, and to value others' perceptions more than your own, then you will need to work on having more empathy for yourself, to stop judging yourself, and to start trusting your perceptions more. You have more than enough empathy for others. You also need to give yourself permission to get angry at those who hurt you (instead of turning that anger in on yourself) and to ask for an apology.

In contrast, if you tend to blame others when something goes wrong and to believe that your perceptions are always right, if you have difficulty admitting when you have made a mistake, and if you have difficulty apologizing for a wrongdoing, you need to work on having more empathy for others, to stop judging others, to start valuing the perceptions of others more, and to apologize when you have harmed others.

What's Your Empathy Style?

Some of you may know your empathy style or may have been able to figure it out from what I've written above, but others may still be confused about it. If this is your situation, start keeping a daily log of your interactions with others. Notice how often you feel others have wronged you and how often you have felt wronged.

A. Make two lists: one noting how many times you catch yourself blaming others when something goes wrong, the other noting how many times you blame yourself when something goes wrong.

B. At the end of a week, notice which list is longer. This will give you a fairly good idea of whether you lack empathy for others or for yourself.

Some Common Excuses for Not Apologizing

The following are the most common excuses we tend to make for not apologizing. Which ones do you relate to the most?

- *It doesn't matter.* Don't fool yourself. It always matters. Think of the times when you wished someone would apologize to you and how hurt you were when that person didn't apologize. Now think of the times when someone did apologize and how good it made you feel. Remember both these feelings the next time you try to convince yourself that it doesn't matter whether you apologize.

- *The person did the same thing to me and didn't apologize.* Two wrongs don't make a right. Maybe the other person didn't realize that he hurt your feelings or made you angry and therefore didn't realize that he had anything to apologize for. Remember that it's your responsibility to ask for an apology, especially if the issue is still bothering you. By apologizing for an inappropriate action, you will actually be letting the other person know that it is hurtful and you will be the role model. The other person may reassess his or her behavior and may be encouraged to apologize in the future.

- *He or she never apologizes to me.* If this is really the case (or are you exaggerating?), then you need to take responsibility by asking for an apology when you feel hurt or offended. You also probably need to have a talk with this person and express your feelings concerning the fact that you don't receive apologies from her. In any case, her behavior is no excuse for insensitive and inconsiderate behavior on your part. Get your revenge by being bigger than the other person and revel in your ability to apologize when she is too proud or unaware.

- *It's too late.* It's never too late for an apology. Although some apologies are far more potent when given shortly after the offense, few people actually reject an apology because it came too late. Let me give you an example from my own life.

Many years ago, I was the clinical director of a counseling center in the Los Angeles area. The executive director of the clinic and I had known each other prior to my being hired, and during my first two years there she and I became quite close. We'd often have dinner together after working late and would spend hours making plans for how to make the clinic function more successfully. I became friends with her son and her boyfriend, and she met all my friends and lovers. One year she had a birthday party for me at her home and one Christmas I brought my mother over to meet her. We confided in each other and we were both there for each other in times of need.

But after about four years, my friend and colleague began to change. She had begun searching for answers for some emotional problems she was experiencing and explored areas outside of psychotherapy. She began to make many new friends and to reach out to them in the way she once had to me. This hurt my feelings, but I was happy that she had found some much-needed support.

What I wasn't happy about was how it began to affect her at work. She stopped asking for my opinions about the direction of the clinic and instead brought in several of her new friends as consultants. Gradually, I began to feel that I had little say in the overall functioning of the clinic, even though I still performed the same job.

I approached her several times to tell her that I felt shut out, but she seemed unwilling to listen. She seemed to be gone from me, as if she had put up a giant wall between us. Unwilling to work under those conditions, I gave her my notice and left the job, telling everyone I wanted to focus full-time on my private practice. Even at my going-away party she remained cold and distant, and this hurt me deeply. We had been through so much together and it hurt to get the cold shoulder from someone I had once been so close to.

For years, whenever I thought about what had happened at the clinic, I felt very sad and very angry. But even though I missed supervising interns and having contact with other therapists, my practice was taking off and I began to write self-help books. In time, I put the entire experience aside and focused on my new life.

Over the next 15 years, I didn't hear from my ex-friend. Then I ran into her at a grocery store 4 hours north of Los Angeles, which was quite a surprise since it was far from where we had once worked together.

Our greeting was understandably awkward. We said hello and she introduced me to the man who was standing close to her. I told her I'd moved to Cambria 5 years earlier and that I loved it there. Then she looked into my eyes and she said, "I'm sorry for hurting you." Once again, I was struck by how powerful those words could be. I could tell by the look on her face and the tone of her voice that she had done some serious thinking about what she'd done to me, and in that moment any vestiges of pain I still held in my heart melted away. I told her I'd forgiven her a long time ago—and in many ways I had. But I was surprised by how much I still needed to hear those words and how healing they were. I was now able to see her humanity. I was now able to recognize the person I had once cared about. And I was now able to regain the respect I once had for her. It had been 15 years since she had hurt me, but it still wasn't too late for an apology.

Why Apology Is Difficult for Some, Easy for Others

Apologizing seems to be far more difficult for some people than it is for others. For example, those who have the hardest time apologizing tend to be:

- Those who were raised to be strong and "macho" and to not show any signs of weakness (often men)

- Perfectionists
- Those who always need to be right
- Those who tend to be very judgmental of others
- Those who tend to project their faults onto others
- Narcissists (they have excessive pride that covers up and protects their fragile egos)
- Those who have been deeply shamed in the past and now have a need to protect themselves from further shaming
- Those who are unable to empathize with others

On the other end of the spectrum are people to whom apologizing seems to come too easily. Those who tend to apologize too often or unnecessarily include:

- Those who are raised to feel they are responsible for *any* misunderstanding, argument, or problem that arises (often women)
- Those who were raised to believe it is a matter of social etiquette to apologize, even when they haven't done anything wrong
- Those who have learned to use apology to manipulate others— either as a way of *appearing* as if they have accepted responsibility for their actions when they haven't or as a way to placate others and convince others to excuse their behavior
- Those who have been victimized and have learned to blame themselves for their own victimization

Those who have been victimized in some way (childhood abuse or neglect, emotional or physical abuse in adult relationships) are prone to overapologizing and apologizing even when they haven't done anything wrong, either in an attempt to keep the peace or due to their shame and guilt regarding the abuse.

The Link Between Pride and Shame

Understanding the link between pride and shame is crucial to understanding why some have difficulty apologizing while others apologize too much. For example, having too much pride or hubris is actually an indication that the person has an issue with shame, possibly from having been severely shamed as a child. Those who have been severely shamed in the past are often incapable of apologizing because it feels the same as being shamed, and they cannot tolerate another such wounding. By the same token, those who apologize too often and those who are unable to ask for an apology also often suffer from issues with shame.

Most of us feel shame when we discover that we have done something to hurt another human being. If it was a relatively small slight, inconvenience, or insult, we likely feel only a tinge of shame. But when we have deeply hurt another person or caused that person considerable distress, shame washes over us like a tidal wave, knocking us off our perch and sometimes burying us under a wall of self-incrimination, remorse, and self-loathing.

We all handle shame differently. Those who have a healthy level of self-esteem and who were not overly shamed as children will tend to bounce back relatively soon from this onslaught of remorse and self-criticism. These same people are also far more likely to apologize for the harm they have caused and are far more likely to be relieved of their shame in the process.

Those with low self-esteem and those who were deeply shamed as children will have a far more difficult time shaking off their shame attack. It will linger on, slowing eroding any vestige of self-confidence they once felt, deeply affecting their self-image. Some of these people can't apologize enough and they feel such deep remorse that even after the apologies, even after they have been exonerated from their sin, the shame lingers on. Others, however, are unable to tolerate the shame that has taken over their psyches. It is as if they are already so filled with shame that there is simply no more room for it. These people are so deeply affected by a shame attack that they immediately construct an emotional wall of steel to protect themselves. This wall goes up so rapidly that it may appear as if they are totally unaffected by the pain of those they have hurt. In fact, the wall can go up so fast that they themselves are unaware of how deeply they have been affected. Needless to say, these are the very people to whom making an apology is extremely difficult, if not impossible.

Why Men Often Have a More Difficult Time Admitting They Are Wrong

There is some truth to the idea that men have a more difficult time apologizing than do women. Experts such as Deborah Tannen, author of *The Argument Culture*, provide ample evidence that there really is a difference between women and men in this regard. A large majority of those who filled out my apology questionnaire said they felt that men have a more difficult time making apologies than women do.

Men generally don't like feeling vulnerable, and to many men apologizing or admitting they are wrong makes them feel far too vulnerable. And many feel that if they apologize, they're losing a power struggle. Men tend to view all disputes, including marital ones, in terms of right and wrong. It logically follows (men tend to be logical) that to be wrong is to lose. And most men hate to lose, especially since they are culturally conditioned to be competitive.

Ironically, some men find apologizing much harder precisely because they know they are wrong. For example, a close friend of mine recently told me:

> When I'm in an argument with my wife and she makes a good point, that's exactly when I pull out the heavy artillery. I'll do things like tell her she's just like her mother or deliberately make her doubt her perceptions by denying I said something I know I did. I do this because I'm panicked and frightened about being proven wrong. I know it seems like no big deal, but to me, at that moment, it feels like I have no power.

Many men have delicate egos. As a male client told me, "I always feel I'm just one mistake away from total failure. I have to keep up this facade of being powerful and being right. Otherwise I'm afraid I'll crumble."

Before we get too critical, let's remember that males in most societies are expected to be strong, competent, and accomplished. As much as women have said they want their men to also be emotional and communicative, they also don't want them to be wimps. If a man were to apologize too often, most women would get turned off.

Why Apologizing Often Comes Too Easily for Women

Research shows that women say they are sorry far more often than men do. Women apologize to their husbands, their friends, their children, their bosses and colleagues, and to people they bump into at the supermarket. They apologize so automatically and so often that they sometimes don't even know why they are apologizing. And often they apologize when a situation isn't their fault.

Why does being a woman mean having to say you're sorry? According to Deborah Tannen, women's tendency to apologize too often is partly a matter of speaking style. She explains that conversation is basically a ritual. We say things because we've learned they are the right things to say in a particular situation. Many of the rituals that women use have the function of taking the other person's feelings into consideration. This is the case with apology. Often when women apologize they are not literally taking responsibility for an action but are merely acknowledging that something may have been difficult for the other person. Unfortunately, "because men are less likely to apologize as an automatic way of being considerate, they may interpret what a woman says as an actual apology," Tannen points out. This tends to leave women in a less powerful position—they may then be seen as weak or inadequate, or they may be assigned blame for things that aren't their fault.

A woman may offer an apology expecting to get one in return (such as when she owns up to her part in a disagreement), but instead her husband may simply view her as always being wrong. A woman who habitually takes (or is given) more than her share of blame in a relationship may come to question her competence and her perceptions. Or she may become more and more enraged. In the traditional man-woman relationship the woman eventually gets angry about the situation—"I'm willing to take responsibility for my part in our problems," one woman told me, "but I'm no longer willing to take it all." When a woman finally erupts, she is often perceived as overreacting, or is labeled irrational or hysterical, and the real substance of her complaint is lost.

Even literal apologies—those given when someone has done, or believes she's done, something wrong—are offered far more often by women than men. Many men learn early on to act strong, self-assured, and independent and to always save face by not admitting fault. But women tend to look at life in a much more personal way. And if a problem arises, particularly if it isn't solved, women tend to feel guilty. They either believe it was somehow their fault or they didn't do enough to solve the problem.

There are four major reasons why women tend to apologize when they are not at fault:

1. Women tend to try to spare the feelings of others.

2. Women tend to blame themselves rather than the situation or the other person.

3. Women tend to have lower self-esteem than men.

4. Women tend to fear and avoid conflict.

Having low self-esteem often translates into constantly feeling apologetic—*I'm sorry for how I look; I'm sorry I get so jealous and insecure; I'm sorry for not being enough; I'm sorry for being who I am*—and frequently taking the blame when not at fault.

Many women will do most anything to avoid conflict, including defusing the situation and avoiding or ending a fight by simply apologizing. This was the situation with one of the women who answered my questionnaire: "My husband almost never apologizes and so I've found that it prevents a lot of arguments if I just take the blame for things."

EXERCISE
Too Much or Too Little

A. Do you have difficulties apologizing or do you apologize too often? Write about why you've gone to one extreme or the other. For example:

1. Were you taught the importance of apology when you were growing up?

2. Were you taught that apologizing was a sign of weakness?

3. What messages did your parents give you, either by their words or example, about apology?

4. Did one or both of your parents commonly use apology as manipulation?

5. Were you ever forced to apologize to someone as a child?

B. For those who have difficulty apologizing, what is most difficult for you about apologizing to another person?

1. How do you feel when you apologize to another person and under what type of circumstances do you think about doing so?

2. Who is the most difficult person for you to apologize to and why?

C. For those who apologize too easily and too often, how do you imagine it would feel if you were to stop yourself from automatically apologizing?

1. Write about what other emotions you might be forced to experience if you didn't automatically apologize.

⚛

We all have reasons why apologizing can be difficult at times. Although it is important to discover some of these, it will not be positive for you to beat yourself up for not apologizing in the past. Instead, remind yourself how important it is to apologize and the power apology has to heal all your relationships.

Apologizing too much and apologizing too little are both problems. Those who apologize too often may lose the respect of others and may be seen as weak and ineffectual. They are often not taken as seriously as they should be. Those who don't apologize as often as they should also lose the respect of others, since they are likely to be seen as inconsiderate, unwilling to take responsibility for their actions, and even as cowards. Clearly a balance needs to be created between the two extremes.

EXERCISE

Revisit Your Apology Lists

Begin this exercise by referring to the two lists you made at the end of Chapter 1.

A. For each person on your first list, ask yourself the following question: Why do you think this person has not apologized to you? Write down your answers. Be as thorough as possible.

B. For each name on your second list, ask yourself the following question: What has stood in the way of your apologizing to this person? Again, write your answers down and elaborate as much as possible. If you can't come up with an answer, spend a little more time thinking about it.

PART TWO

⚛

Learn How to Give a Meaningful Apology

CHAPTER 4

The Right and Wrong Way to Apologize

*If you tell the truth, you have infinite power supporting you;
but if not, you have infinite power against you.*

CHARLES GORDON

Excuses are always mixed with lies.

ARAB PROVERB

THE POWER OF APOLOGY PRINCIPLE 4
A meaningful apology communicates the three R's: regret, responsibility, and remedy.

I n this chapter, I explain in detail how to make a *meaningful, heartfelt* apology that is healing for both you and the person to whom you are apologizing.

Let's begin by discussing the wrong way to apologize—those types of apologies that tend to be less effective than others. Then I will explain the right way to make a meaningful apology.

Meaningless Apologies

Some types of apology are clearly ineffective and even meaningless. In this section, many of these are examined, along with some case examples.

The Fake or False Apology

We've all received these types of apologies and many of us have given them. Fake apologies are often the perfunctory apologies given in social and business situations, or in situations where an apology is expected even when it is not genuinely felt.

Although it is important for children to be taught apology, often parents make the mistake of insisting that children give apologies when they don't really understand what they have done wrong or when they feel they haven't done anything wrong. In many cases, this sets the stage for many of us to continue making fake apologies when we become adults.

A false apology can be likened to a lie. The person giving a false apology is usually doing so in an attempt to manipulate the person he or she has offended into being forgiving. We've all had the experience of being charmed into forgiving someone, even though we didn't really feel the person was genuinely sorry, but our forgiveness is usually about as genuine as the apology. Our trust hasn't really been regained and our resentment usually creeps back in before long. The apology President Clinton made concerning Monica Lewinsky may come to mind when we think about false apologies.

The Apology Delivered to Evade Punishment or Disfavor

Often we apologize merely to avoid negative reactions from others. In reality, we aren't sorry for the harm we caused but for getting caught.

For many years, I have specialized in working with adult survivors of childhood abuse, their partners, and their families. In relatively few cases have the parents of abuse victims admitted their actions. When they do, they usually do not believe their actions were abusive. This is particularly true of perpetrators of childhood sexual abuse, as is evident in the following case.

Jenny's father sexually abused her from the time she was 4 years old until she was 16. He would come into her room at night and fondle her under the guise of soothing her so that she could sleep better. This went on for several years before he also began to have her fondle him. By the time she was reaching puberty, he was having intercourse with her.

After many years of therapy, Jenny was finally able to confront her father about the abuse. Unlike most perpetrators, her father admitted his actions even though he minimized them and denied that they could have caused her problems. When she tried to explain how the abuse had profoundly affected her, he merely pointed out how successful she was (she had, in fact, become a doctor) and that the abuse must not have harmed her that much.

For several years after her confrontation with him, Jenny continued her relationship with her father even though she was uncomfortable around him. She felt proud of herself for confronting him and she rationalized to herself that he had, after all, admitted the abuse, which was something she hadn't expected.

I met Jenny when she joined a group I was leading for female survivors of childhood abuse. Since she'd done everything the books and her previous therapist had recommended to maximize the recovery process, she didn't understand why she was so depressed and why she still felt unfinished business with her father. When I tried to get her to express anger toward her father, she always made excuses for his behavior and even tended to question what role she might have played in her own abuse. She was a strong advocate for forgiving and forgetting and was angry at herself because she couldn't seem to do either one. It was clear to me that Jenny needed to get to the anger that lay buried underneath her tendency to be overly empathetic and compassionate.

With the support of the other women in the group, Jenny became more and more angry at her father and less and less willing to blame herself. Then one day, after working with me for almost a year, Jenny asked me if I would be willing to conduct a session with her and her father. She explained, "I feel stronger now and I think I'll be able to stand up for myself a lot better than I did before. I want to tell him again how much he hurt me and how much his behavior has negatively affected my life. I want him to really hear me and I want him to apologize to me."

I spent several individual sessions preparing Jenny for this most important meeting, spelling out the possible consequences and coaching her on how to be more assertive. I felt confident that she would do well, even though from her description of her father I was also prepared for a hostile, almost pathologically defensive man and didn't have much hope that he would really hear her, accept full responsibility for his actions, or apologize.

Sure enough, Jenny's father matched her description of him precisely. The man was so defensive that when I looked at him it was as if there were no one home. His real self was hidden behind a powerfully strong emotional wall.

Jenny started out by thanking her father for coming and I echoed her sentiments, stating that it took a great deal of courage for him to do so. He brushed both our comments aside and insisted that he would do anything to help his daughter.

Jenny then began telling her father how the abuse had negatively affected her life. He immediately started contradicting her, reminding her that her mother's treatment of her hadn't been all that great either, and saying such things as "what doesn't kill us makes us stronger."

Jenny told him she didn't want to hear his excuses. She wanted him to be quiet and listen. He blinked, shrugged his shoulders, and fell silent. Although he allowed Jenny to finish without interrupting her, it was obvious her words weren't sinking in. He was just biding his time until the whole thing was over.

After Jenny finished, she looked at her father and said, "Now I want an apology from you." Her father immediately jumped in with, "How many times do I have to tell you I'm sorry? I don't know what you want from me. I've told you over and over, but it never seems to be enough for you. I can't take back what I've done. Why do you let it continue to bother you? It was years ago. You're an adult woman now. It's time to get over it."

His words were very effective and they silenced Jenny for several minutes. But Jenny wasn't about to give up. "I'll never get over it, Dad. That's the point. But in order for me to continue having a relationship with you, I need to know you understand how much you damaged me and I need you to apologize like you really mean it."

Realizing that his daughter probably meant what she said about not continuing to see him unless he apologized, Jenny's father said, "I am sorry. I'm sorry. I'm sorry. I'm sorry. I wish it had never happened. Who wants to keep going through this torture?"

Jenny had not received a genuine, heartfelt apology. Her father's words were absolutely meaningless to her. As she explained to me later, she realized in that moment that he would never really apologize because he was incapable of having any empathy for her and her pain. It was all about him. It was all about trying to appease her so that she'd continue to see him. It was all about trying to appear to be the good father who would do anything for his daughter, while all along he was just thinking about himself. In addition to not wanting his daughter to stop seeing him, her father was also afraid that Jenny would tell other family members, including her brothers, about what he had done. Therefore, he would appease her by going to therapy, by apologizing, or by doing anything else she asked in order to avoid exposure.

The Apology Without Remorse

Obviously the apology without remorse is similar to the apology given to avoid punishment or disfavor, since the person who apologizes to avoid consequences generally does not feel true remorse. This was the case with the apology that my client, Robin, received from her boss at work.

For several months after beginning her new job, Robin endured inappropriate comments from her boss concerning the way she dressed, her body, and her sex life. If she dressed up a little more than usual, he would say something like, "Oh, you look sexy today. I'll bet you have a hot date tonight, right? That lucky dog." If her blouse was slightly low-cut, her skirt the least bit short, or a dress slightly tight, he would leer at her, wet his lips, and say something like, "If I wasn't a married man . . . " or "How do you expect me to get any work done with you dressed like that?"

These comments bothered Robin so much that she started dressing far more conservatively than was her preferred style, hoping this would cut down on such remarks. In response, her boss said, "What happened? Where's the sexy secretary I hired? What have you done with her? Who's this frumpy person who has taken her place?"

Robin felt she couldn't win. If she dressed nicely, she got his inappropriate comments. If she dressed down, she was criticized by him. Deeply upset, she finally went to the employee relations representative at her firm and made a complaint. While the employee relations person took her report, she encouraged Robin to participate in a mediation session between her and her boss in lieu of filing a formal sexual harassment charge. Robin agreed.

At the meeting, her boss formally apologized for speaking to her in an inappropriate way. "I'm sorry if I offended you in any way, Miss Cravens. It was not my intent to do so. I assure you I will not make any such comments in the future," he said very formally, looking over her left shoulder.

Robin had received an apology without remorse. Her boss was clearly just mouthing words that his lawyer had no doubt instructed him to say. There was no sign of regret in his voice. Robin left the meeting feeling very unsatisfied. And although the inappropriate comments did stop, her boss made it clear by his body language and icy silence that he felt she had made a big deal out of nothing.

The Bitter Apology

The bitter apology is often delivered through clenched teeth. Most people who give a bitter apology feel forced to do so in order to avoid negative consequences. As with Jenny and her father, it may have been made clear that unless an apology was forthcoming, the relationship would end. It is evident to all concerned that the person is not only unremorseful for his or her actions but resents having to apologize. This makes the apology not only meaningless but insulting.

The Premature Apology

An apology is premature if sufficient time has not been taken to consider fully the consequences of the wrongdoing. An apology that is given without thought or feeling is meaningless and empty.

Most people would rather receive a genuine, heartfelt apology that took many hours, months, or even years than one that came within seconds of an offense and was given with no thought or feeling.

Premature apologies are often given when we suddenly become aware that we have offended another person and wish to, in essence, take back the offense. Thinking that an immediate apology might act as a way to erase the offense and appease the offended, we apologize quickly and enthusiastically, often with a flair or flourish. Unfortunately, because the apology comes so fast, the offended party usually doesn't trust it, or the person giving it. A good example is when we say something hurtful to someone and then immediately try to take it back by saying we were just kidding or that we really didn't mean it. This leaves the other person wondering not only how sincere our apology was but why we said the hurtful thing in the first place. A more appropriate way to handle this situation is to apologize for any hurt feelings and to possibly say, "Gee, I wonder where that came from? I'm going to have to think about that for a while."

The Self-Blaming Apology

The self-blaming apology is meant to disarm the offended party and take the focus off the offense. The self-blamer will overapologize and then exaggerate the offense, for example, "I'm so terribly sorry. What an idiot. I can't believe I did such a stupid thing. I don't blame you if you never speak to me again. I could just kick myself."

The self-blamer cleverly manages to make the offended party feel sorry for him for being so hard on himself. Not only do most people temporarily forget about the offense, but they end up taking care of the person who is apologizing. This nullifies the apology entirely.

The "Political" Apology

Political apologies are made either in an attempt to look good to others (because it is the politically correct thing to do) or to gain favors from others. They are apologies of *expedience* versus those of *substance*. Often those in business will make a show of apologizing for something (usually in front of others) in an attempt to impress others with their sense of honor or fairness, or in an attempt to disarm those from whom an attack is imminent.

For example, Dr. Laura Schlessinger took out a full-page ad in *Variety* apologizing to gays for her harsh words against them. Although this came on the Day of Atonement for the Jewish people, spokespersons for gay and lesbian organizations didn't buy it. Her show had just been canceled in Canada and it seemed like a ploy to save her show in the United States. And Robert McNamara finally admitted the United States was wrong to be involved in Vietnam (though he didn't actually say "I'm sorry"), but he did so when it was useful in promoting his book.

The Angry Apology

The angry apology occurs when we either attempt to apologize too soon or we secretly blame the other person for causing us to behave as we did. A new acquaintance of mine recently told me that his ex-wife had become very angry with him for divulging what she considered to be a family secret in his annual Christmas letter. He tried to e-mail her an apology, but he received a message that she wasn't accepting any e-mails from him at this time. Angry and hurt by her rejection, he called her. He began by apologizing for his Christmas letter, but then he told her that he resented the fact that she hadn't accepted his e-mail. Frustrated and angry, she yelled, "That's exactly why I didn't want an e-mail from you. I knew you couldn't apologize without blaming me somehow."

When we talked about what had happened, it became apparent that he shouldn't have attempted an apology at the time for two reasons: (1) He was angry with his ex-wife for getting mad at him about the Christmas letter in the first place. Throughout their marriage she had made a big thing about keeping family secrets, and he personally didn't feel he'd done anything wrong by divulging this particular information. When his ex-wife refused to accept his e-mail, he was further angered. (2) During their marriage he never experienced his wife taking responsibility for anything she did wrong. Although he was sorry he'd upset her and wanted to communicate this, on some level he resented apologizing to her when she would not do the same.

Bumbled Apologies

Often, even when our intentions are good, our apologies come across as less than sincere. When this happens, the other person may actually become more hurt or angered by our bumbling attempt. In order to avoid making this mistake, avoid making these types of apologies:

- *The conditional apology ("I'm sorry, but . . .").* In essence, the conditional apology conveys the message that you aren't willing to take full responsibility for your actions. Conditional apologies often imply that you wouldn't have done what you did if it weren't for someone else's actions (including the person you hurt). This type of apology may even give the impression that you aren't entirely sorry for what you did but are merely going through the motions. Here are a few famous conditional apologies:

    Sorry but—"Well, I'm sorry I didn't sing so good, but I'd like to hear him sing it" (Roseanne, after President Bush called her

1990 rendition of the national anthem at a San Diego Padres baseball game "disgraceful").

In fairness to me—"I acknowledge that in the past I have, on occasion, made insensitive remarks which I now realize hurt others. . . . I am profoundly sorry and I apologize to anyone I hurt. . . . In fairness to me, I wish to add that . . . minority issues have been present in baseball long before I came to the game" (Cincinnati Reds owner Marge Schott, after being accused in 1992 of making racist and anti-Semitic remarks).

However—"When I reflect on the pain I caused Mrs. Buttafuoco, her children, and my own family, I can accept and understand my imprisonment. However, . . . if Mr. Buttafuoco had permitted me to cross the bridge between adolescence and adulthood unmolested, I would not be where I am today" (Amy Fisher, at Joey Buttafuoco's 1993 sentencing for statutory rape).

- *The half-apology ("I'm sorry you feel bad").* This type of apology is usually perceived as a cop-out, since it is an obvious attempt on the apologizer's part to avoid taking responsibility for his or her actions. Women in particular complain that their husbands and boyfriends attempt to apologize in this way, and they experience it as more irritating than helpful. It makes people angry to realize that you either have too much pride to make a full apology or that you are unable to admit when you are wrong.

Other Common Reasons for Failed Apologies

In addition to the previous examples of bumbled apologies, the following are two of the most common reasons why apologies fail. As you read them, think about whether they might have played a part in a bumbled apology of yours or had a role in your being unable to forgive someone even though he or she apologized.

- *The wrongdoer trivializes the damage he or she may have caused.* A wrongdoer can trivialize her behavior by making it clear that she feels an apology is not really in order, by clearly expressing an insincere attitude, or in an extreme case by possibly saying, "It really wasn't any big deal, but I know you aren't going to forgive me until I apologize, so here it is: 'I'm sorry.'" This apology is offensive.

- *The timing is wrong.* For a minor offense such as accidentally spilling coffee on someone, if you don't apologize right away the offense becomes personal and grows in magnitude. The more time that passes, the more offended the other person becomes that you didn't have the decency to apologize.

In general, apologies are most effective when they are given when the event is current, not after a great deal of time has passed. As a case in point, let's compare the effectiveness of the 1995 apology by the Southern Baptist Convention for their pro-slavery stand and for the racism that defined them for many years with the 1991 apology by the Dutch Reformed Church to South Africans for having provided religious justification for apartheid. Although both apologies were considered sincere, the Afrikaners had something more going for them. They apologized when their country was in the grip of a turbulent transition. They made their voices heard when they counted, and it seemed to help. The Baptists offered their apology more than 30 years after the height of the civil rights struggle. One can only imagine the impact had they repented when it mattered most.

On the other hand, it is often better late than never in many situations, such as in the case of parents who abused their children when they were growing up. For a more serious offense, such as a betrayal of trust (e.g., having an extramarital affair or telling a friend's secret when you promised you wouldn't), an immediate apology may actually feel insulting to the other person. It may indicate that you haven't taken time to consider the magnitude of the offense or that you are trivializing the offense by expecting the other person to get over it right away just because you apologized. With more serious offenses, it is the care and thought that goes into the apology that dignifies the exchange. Furthermore, days, weeks, or even months may go by before both parties can fully integrate the meaning of the event and its impact on the relationship.

When It Is Appropriate to Apologize and When It Isn't

As in many of the cases described in this chapter, when an apology is not heartfelt, when it is done to placate another person or to make yourself look good, the words are literally meaningless. In addition, you should never apologize:

- Just because you feel it is expected of you. Apologies must be voluntary. There must be a genuine desire to make amends.
- Because someone else feels that you should.
- Because you just want the whole issue to be over with and apologizing seems to be the quickest way to resolve it.
- When you are still angry.
- When you simply aren't ready to apologize.
- When you don't really think you did anything that was inappropriate, insensitive, or wrong.
- When you just want to make someone else feel better, even though you feel you've done nothing wrong.

You should never apologize unless you feel you did something that requires an apology. If in your heart you feel that what you did was justified, or was a result of what the other person did, then you should not apologize.

Others can tell whether you are making a sincere apology, whether your apology is coming from your heart, or whether it is merely lip service. (Remember the reaction many people had to President Clinton's apology concerning Monica Lewinsky.)

Even more important, unless you are ready and willing to accept complete responsibility and to admit you were wrong, you will not receive the benefits of your apology.

When Apologizing Can Be Unhealthy

In some instances, apologizing can even be unhealthy. Consider the following situation.

Maria, a woman in one of my groups for emotionally abused women, felt compelled to apologize to her ex-husband for having an affair at the end of their marriage. She explained that even though her ex-husband had been emotionally abusive to her throughout their marriage and ending the marriage had become necessary for her mental health, she always felt guilty about the affair and wanted to apologize to him.

A few weeks after her apology, her ex-husband called her late at night wanting phone sex. Still afraid of his reaction if she were to reject him, she cajoled him by reminding him that he had a girl-friend who would most certainly be hurt by his actions. This seemed to work and he hung up.

But several nights later, he called again. She once again reminded him that his behavior would hurt his girlfriend, but this time he wasn't so quick to hang up. Instead he tried pressuring her. It was obvious to Maria that her apology had been taken as an invitation to resume abusing her (throughout their marriage he'd pressured her sexually) and that apologizing to him had been a mistake.

Maria's experience is an excellent example of when apologizing can be unhealthy. Generally speaking, it is best to forgo apologizing directly to the other person:

- If the apology will be misconstrued as an invitation to rekindle a relationship you struggled long and hard to remove yourself from

- If your apology will likely feel like an invitation to abuse you further

- If an apology is likely to be used as an excuse to blame you for all the problems in the relationship

- If your apology will be used against you in any way

- If by apologizing you cause yourself to become dangerously vulnerable

How to Give a Meaningful Apology

A meaningful apology communicates the three R's: regret, responsibility, and remedy:

Regret—A statement of regret for having caused the inconvenience, hurt, or damage. This includes an expression of empathy toward the other person, including an acknowledgment of the inconvenience, hurt, or damage that you caused the other person.

Having empathy for the person you hurt or angered is the most important part of your apology. When you truly have empathy, the other person will feel it. Your apology will wash over him or her like a healing balm. If you don't have empathy, your apology will sound and feel empty.

Responsibility—An acceptance of responsibility for your actions. This means not blaming anyone else for what you did and not making excuses for your actions but instead accepting full responsibility for what you did and for the consequences of your actions.

Remedy—A statement of your willingness to take action to remedy the situation—either by promising not to repeat your action, promising to work toward not making the same mistake again, stating how you are going to remedy the situation (e.g., go to therapy), or making restitution for the damages you caused.

Apologizing to your spouse for having an affair is insulting unless you offer reassurances: *It will never happen again because we will seek therapy, because I've quit my job, because I'll take you on my business trips.*

Regret, Responsibility, and Remedy

Unless all three of these elements are present, the other person will sense that something is missing in your apology and he or she will feel shortchanged somehow. Let's take a look at each element in more detail with examples.

Regret

The desire to apologize needs to come from the realization that you have hurt someone or caused that person some difficulty. While your intention may not have been to hurt this person, you recognize that your action or inaction nevertheless did hurt or inconvenience him, and you feel bad. This regret or remorse needs to be communicated to the other person. For example:

- "I am so sorry. I know I hurt your feelings and I feel terrible about it."
- "I deeply regret having hurt you."
- "I am truly sorry for the pain I caused you."

Responsibility

For an apology to be effective, it must be clear that you are accepting total responsibility for your actions or inaction. Therefore, your apology needs to include a statement of responsibility. For example:

- "I'm sorry. I realize that by being late I made us miss the first part of the movie."

- "I'm sorry. I know it is difficult for you to trust people, and my lying to you hasn't made it any easier. I shouldn't have lied no matter how afraid I was of your reaction."

- "I'm sorry. You have every right to be angry with me. I shouldn't have said those words to you."

- "I'm so sorry. There's no excuse for my behavior and I know I hurt you deeply."

Remedy

Although you can't go back and undo or redo the past, you can do everything within your power to repair the harm you caused. Therefore, a meaningful apology needs to include a statement in which you offer restitution in some way—an offer to help the other person, or a promise to take action so that you will not repeat the behavior. For example:

- "I'm sorry. Let me make it up to you. Next time the movie is on me."

- "I'm sorry for lying to you. I promise I won't do it again."

- "I'm sorry for talking to you like that. I'll work on letting you know when I don't like something instead of holding it all in and then exploding like that."

- "I'm sorry. I'm going to go into therapy so that I can understand why I act the way I do."

Intention and Attitude

The two most important underlying aspects of an apology are your intention and your attitude. These will be communicated nonverbally to the person to whom you are apologizing. If your apology does not come from a sincere attempt on your part to express your heartfelt feelings of regret, to take responsibility for your actions, and to right the wrong you've caused, your apology will not feel meaningful or believable to the other person.

In order for the person you have wronged to feel this sincerity, your desire to apologize must come from inside you. You should never attempt an apology just because someone else tells you it is the right thing to do, because you know the other person is expecting it, or because you know it will get you what you want from the other person. Apologies that are given as mere social gestures will likely come across as empty and meaningless. Apologies that are mere manipulations to get what you want will likely be spotted for what they are.

Make No Excuses

Once you begin to reconstruct what led up to the wrongdoing, it is natural to begin making excuses for your actions. While there may be valid reasons for your behavior, there is no excuse. It is important that you realize the difference.

Owning up to the wrong you've done isn't easy, especially when the person you've harmed has also wronged you. But no matter what you've done, most people respond positively to honesty. Admit your mistake; acknowledge that you messed up. By owning up to the fact that you harmed someone, by refusing to make excuses for your actions, you will engender respect from the person you've harmed. By apologizing for your actions, you will encourage forgiveness.

The Six Steps Before You Apologize

In order to make a meaningful apology, you must first complete the following steps. Otherwise, your apology is likely to be weak and ineffective.

Step 1: Admit Your Offense to Yourself

You can't feel true remorse unless you admit to yourself that what you did was wrong. And if you can't be honest with yourself, you certainly aren't going to be able to be honest with the person you offended when you attempt to apologize.

Have a conversation with yourself in which you are brutally honest about the situation, or write a letter confronting yourself about what you did. Don't whitewash. Don't make excuses. Don't blame others. Take complete responsibility for your actions or inaction. This will not only prepare you to make a more meaningful apology but will help you to learn from your mistakes.

Step 2: Take Time to Consider the Ramifications of Your Action or Inaction

An important aspect of taking full responsibility for your actions is to carefully consider the effects that your actions or inaction had on others. Begin by asking yourself how your behavior affected the other person's life. For example, do you feel the person may have difficulties trusting others in the future? Do you feel your actions may have affected this person's self-esteem? Sometimes our actions or inactions affect more than one person. If this is the case, take time to consider the effects on each person involved.

Step 3: Put Yourself in the Place of the Person You Wronged and Try to Understand How He or She Felt

One of the best ways of discovering how your action or inaction may have affected the other person is to look at the situation from the other person's perspective. Imagine how he or she felt because of your action or inaction. Really put yourself in the other person's place. Was he or she angry? Hurt? Disappointed? Once again, be honest with yourself and don't minimize the situation.

If you have difficulty putting yourself in the other person's place, don't get discouraged. Many people have difficulty empathizing with others. The more you work at it, the more empathy you will develop. Try pretending you are the other person and talk out loud about how the situation affected you. Or write about the situation from the other person's point of view.

Step 4: Forgive Yourself

Apologizing to the person you hurt or harmed will no doubt help you to forgive yourself, especially if he or she is able to forgive you. But, paradoxically, you will need to begin the process of forgiving yourself if your apology is to be effective. If you approach the person you wronged feeling overwhelmed with guilt, you will be distracted from where your focus needs to be—on the person you wronged and his or her feelings.

Real guilt is a necessary social emotion. It is our conscience's way of preventing us from doing things we will later regret. Our society would fall apart if we were incapable of feeling real guilt. It is felt when we have violated our own moral code.

If you do something on your own volition, without coercion or intimidation, that you know is morally wrong, then you will suffer real, healthy guilt. While real guilt can serve a positive function in our society, holding onto your guilt does not serve a positive function. The most effective way of relieving your guilt and of forgiving yourself is to make certain that you do not repeat the offense again.

Step 5: Forgive the Person to Whom You Are Apologizing

You will find it impossible to make sincere apologies to others for your side of a conflict unless you have forgiven them for the harms they have caused you. Even if you don't bring up the other person's mistakes directly, your ill will toward him or her will come through in other ways.

Rose, a dear friend of mine, has dedicated the past 10 years to her spiritual growth. One of the most important aspects of this growth has been to make amends to all those with whom she has had conflicts or misunderstandings. To her, this has meant sitting down with each person she has hurt. Throughout the years, she has had meetings with her grown children, her ex-husband, her brothers, and some of her friends. At each meeting she has apologized to the person for her hurtful behavior or attitude and has asked them to forgive her.

These were difficult encounters for my friend, who admittedly tends to be extremely proud and often defensive. At times it took all the courage she could muster in order to actually go through with it. But she felt she was being guided by God to make these amends and she felt it was important for her spiritual growth, so she persevered even when she doubted her strength.

Recently, she told me that she had come to the realization that she needed to make amends to her ex-husband's new wife, Margaret. Even though Margaret had maliciously gossiped about her and tried to turn Rose's children against her, Rose was now painfully aware that she too had acted hurtfully and maliciously toward Margaret. In response to Margaret's behavior, my friend had stooped to her level and had repeatedly said negative things about her to others. I was absolutely astounded that Rose had come to this place in her spiritual growth. And yet she wasn't doing it without trepidation. "This is going to be one of the hardest things I have ever done in my life," she told me. "I feel it is important to do, but there is a part of me that continues to resist it. I keep thinking of the horrible things she's said about me in the past and I get angry all over again. I just hope my anger doesn't come up while I'm trying to make amends."

My advice to her was that she needed to work more on forgiving this person; otherwise her amends would not be effective. While some people need to focus more on releasing their anger, in Rose's case this didn't seem to be working. Instead she found that praying for Margaret helped her get past her resentments. For several weeks prior to their meeting, she asked God to bless her former enemy. She also prayed for help in removing her anger. By the time she met with Margaret, she was far more forgiving and was able to apologize for her part in the relationship without being distracted by resentments. Much to her surprise, Margaret accepted her apology wholeheartedly and apologized in turn for her part in the relationship. They are now on friendly terms and actually get together at some family gatherings, making Rose's children's lives a lot easier.

Unless you completely forgive the person you wronged for his or her part in the interaction, your resentment will seep out and contaminate your apology. The entire process will be sabotaged.

Step 6: Plan and Prepare for Your Apology

Making an apology is a very serious thing. Therefore, it is very important that you plan and prepare for your apology in order to maximize the possibilities of it being a positive experience for both you and the person you wronged.

Impulsively picking up the phone or going to someone's house to apologize can set you up for disappointment. You need to devote time to thinking about the consequences of your actions and to empathize with the person you harmed. And you need to give some thought about what you want to say. There will, of course, be occasions when a spontaneous "I'm sorry" is very appropriate. But for those bigger mistakes and transgressions, impulsiveness and spontaneity may convey disrespect and may cause you to botch your efforts at apology. We don't often get a second chance at an apology, so make the best of your efforts by preparing yourself.

On the other hand, don't allow yourself to become so obsessed with what you are going to say and how you are going to say it that you become immobilized.

Choosing How to Deliver Your Apology

The manner in which you apologize can be as important as the apology itself. For example, some people choose to apologize in person, whereas others feel that it is more advantageous to apologize in writing. In this section I discuss the various ways in which you may choose to apologize, along with the pros and cons of each.

Face-to-Face Apologies

A face-to-face apology is usually best because it affords the opportunity for the wronged person to see your face and thus be better able to ascertain your sincerity. But it takes courage to look the person you wronged directly in the eyes, admit your offense, and apologize. And it takes courage to have the person you wronged look in your eyes and see your vulnerability and remorse. If you have this courage, you will benefit tremendously. Whether the other person is able to forgive you or not, you'll feel good about yourself for being able to face up to your mistakes.

There can, however, be some disadvantages to a face-to-face apology. The person being apologized to may feel as if he or she is put on the spot and is being pressured to forgive. You may want to preface your apology by saying, "I would like to apologize to you for . . . I don't expect you to be ready to forgive me. I just want to say my piece and then I'll give you time to think about what I've said."

A face-to-face apology should never be attempted if you have any reason to suspect that the person you wronged may lash out at you physically. If you know ahead of time that this person tends to act out violently and is still extremely angry with you, it is probably not a good idea to apologize face-to-face.

Written Apologies

Some people feel compelled to travel great distances in order to apologize in person. If this is your situation, by all means follow your instincts. But in most cases a written apology is probably your best option if the person you wronged lives very far away from you.

Written apologies are a good choice for those who tend to bumble attempts at speaking from the heart. Some people just don't do well at expressing themselves verbally, either because they become very nervous or they don't think well under pressure. Writing your apology down on paper will likely be far less stressful to you and can be more effective as well.

A written apology can also feel like less pressure to the person you are apologizing to than a face-to-face apology. It gives the person you wronged plenty of time and space to decide whether he or she is prepared to forgive you. He can reread your letter at leisure, affording him the opportunity to think through the situation completely.

Be sure to keep a copy of your apology letter in case the person you've wronged wants to discuss it with you or has questions about what you wrote. It can also be a good idea to keep a copy of the letter as a reminder of the consequences your words and actions can have on others and yourself.

Some people hesitate writing their apologies down on paper because it feels too threatening to expose their mistakes and vulnerability in black and white, but for many it is exactly what they need to do. It is much harder to remain in denial about the negative consequences of inappropriate or hurtful behavior when it is staring at you from a piece of paper.

E-mail Apologies

Many of us have become quite skilled at writing e-mails and prefer this form of correspondence to other means. If this is your situation, as well as that of the person to whom you wish to apologize, an e-mail apology can be a positive option.

As with an apology that is written and mailed, an e-mail apology provides the person receiving it the time to digest your apology fully before feeling that he or she needs to respond. Just make sure you preface your e-mail apology with a statement giving the other person permission to take his or her time in responding, since most people generally answer their e-mails right away.

Taped Apologies

For those who live far away from the person they wronged but who have difficulty writing down their feelings, taping their apology is a good option. Taping gives you the chance to edit and reedit until you are able to say exactly what you want. And in spite of the distance, listening to a tape of your voice can make what could be an otherwise impersonal experience far more meaningful. As with written apologies, taping your apology gives the person you wronged the option of listening to the tape more than once, allowing your words to sink in and giving him or her the time and space to decide whether he or she is ready to forgive you.

Phone Apologies

Phone apologies are probably the least effective. The person you wronged doesn't have the benefit of ascertaining your sincerity by the expression on your face, or the benefit of being able to reread a letter or e-mail or replay a tape. He may feel pressured to decide on the spot whether he is ready to forgive you, and you have no way of gauging his reaction other than the tone of his voice. If at all possible, choose one of the other methods of apology over this one.

Rehearsing Your Apology and Planning Your Restitution

It is best to rehearse your apology before actually giving it. If you are going to do it face-to-face, on a tape recorder, or by phone, practice what you plan on saying by speaking the words out loud to yourself or into a tape recorder. If you plan on writing out your apology, make a few rough drafts before completing your final version. Since this will probably be your only chance to apologize to this person, put thought and effort into it. It will pay off.

Another important aspect of your preparation is to think about how you plan to make restitution for the harm you caused. If you caused damage to or destroyed someone's property, come up with a plan for how you will repair the damage.

There are, of course, situations in which restitution seems difficult, if not impossible. For example, you can't take back cruel or negative gossip, you can't undo physical or emotional abuse, and there is no obvious restitution for infidelity. While exact restitution is sometimes impossible, if you put your mind to it you can come up with creative ideas on how some form of restitution can be made. In the case of cruel or negative gossip, you can make every effort to clear up negative impressions you created about a person. In the case of emotional or physical abuse, you can enter therapy or a support group to make sure you do not abuse anyone again, and you can donate your time or money to organizations that work to help victims of abuse. In the case of infidelity, you can enter individual therapy or marriage counseling in order to discover why you were unfaithful and to make certain you do not repeat the offense.

Prepare Yourself for Any Outcome

It is important to prepare yourself for any result when you apologize. The person you wronged may enthusiastically accept your apology and may even thank you for being so forthcoming and for making him or her feel good. The person you apologize to may let you know that he or she now respects you more due to the courage you showed in accepting responsibility. A severed friendship may be mended, your marriage may be strengthened, or you may even forestall a legal action pending against you.

On the other hand, the person you have wronged may tell you that she is unable to forgive you, or that even though she accepts your apology, it is going to take a great deal of time before she can once again trust you, or that although she accepts your apology she no longer wishes to have any kind of relationship with you.

You will also need to be prepared for the other person's anger. Just because you've had the courage to apologize doesn't mean you automatically wipe away the consequences of your actions. In fact, apologizing for the wrong you did may open the door to weeks, months, or years of anger on the part of the person you've wronged. And don't assume that your specific apology will cover all your offenses. The other person may bring up additional offenses of which you may or may not be aware.

By being prepared for any outcome you won't be as devastated if you receive one of these latter responses. If someone is not willing to forgive you, accept it as a strong reminder that your words and actions have consequences, including those of causing great injury to others and severing important relationships.

Whether the person you apologize to is able to forgive you isn't half as important as the fact that you were able to admit your wrong to the person you harmed. This act in itself will be healing to you, no matter what the outcome. You will be freed from the guilt and shame you've been carrying around, and you will gain self-respect because you were willing and able to take responsibility for your actions.

PART THREE

Learn How to Receive and Accept Apologies

CHAPTER 5

Opening the Door
with Empathy

Only my condemnation injures me.
Only my own forgiveness sets me free.

THE COURSE IN MIRACLES

If you offend, ask for pardon; if offended, forgive.

ETHIOPIAN PROVERB

One who has begged for forgiveness should not be so cruel as
not to forgive.

RASHI

THE POWER OF APOLOGY PRINCIPLE 5

In order to truly forgive, most people need to gain empathy and compassion for the wrongdoer.

Making an apology can be difficult, but being on the receiving end can be just as difficult. We're supposed to forgive and forget. But the hurt can linger a lot longer than it takes to say "I'm sorry," and the damage can sometimes be so severe that "I'm sorry" doesn't seem to be enough. We often want more. Some want revenge, while others want restitution. Some want the offending party to suffer or at least to spend a great deal of time groveling, while others want an assurance that the person has truly learned from the experience and has changed.

The Opening of a Door

It's important to realize that "I'm sorry" doesn't have to signal the end of the discussion; in fact, in many cases, it should mean only the beginning. Think of an apology as the opening of a door. You can choose to walk through the door to another room where you and the wrongdoer can sit down and talk.

The ideal situation is a sincere apology, followed by a gracious acceptance and a healing discussion. There are several things you, the recipient of the apology, can do to make the apology more personally meaningful, as well as to make it more possible for you to gain closure. Try the following suggestions:

- Don't bottle up your feelings just because the other person apologized. If you are still angry or hurt, say so.
- Don't assume you should be ready to forgive just because the other person apologized. Forgiveness often takes time.
- Don't expect an apology to resolve the underlying reason why a person did something. If you feel the other person's actions had meaning that needs to be understood, suggest a further discussion. For example, you might say, "I accept your apology, but I'd like to talk further about why you did what you did," or "I appreciate the apology, but I still have a problem with what you did."
- Don't accept an apology just to make the other person feel better.
- Don't accept what you experience as an insincere apology. Instead, suggest that you have a discussion about why the apologist did what he or she did or how he or she can avoid repeating the behavior.

When You Have Difficulty Letting in an Apology

Have you ever received a heartfelt apology only to brush it away as if it were meaningless? I certainly have.

Many people have difficulty receiving apologies. For some, it is

because they tend to take on too much responsibility for ou.
actions or to minimize their own pain and suffering. Others have as
much difficulty accepting an apology as they do accepting a com-
pliment because they have difficulty taking in good things.

Sometimes an apology catches us off guard and we don't know
how to respond. Remember the friend and business associate who
apologized for her behavior toward me when I met her in a store?
When she apologized to me, I was caught so unexpectedly that all
I could say was, "I forgave you a long time ago. I'm sorry for my part
in it too." Although these two statements were true, they weren't
really what I wanted to say. I wanted to tell her how much I'd
needed that apology, how much it meant to me. Even though I had
actually forgiven her long ago, I still needed to hear those words. I
still needed to know she was sorry. Telling her I was sorry for my
part in the problems somehow took away from the courage she'd
shown by apologizing. I wished I'd waited a few minutes, let the
apology sink in, then told her how much I appreciated it. After that
part of the exchange was complete, it would have been far more
appropriate for me to apologize to her.

This was a good lesson for me. Since then, when I receive an
apology, no matter what it is for, I take the time to let it in. This is
what I suggest you do: Take a deep breath and let the apology in.
Let it sink into your mind and into your heart. Allow yourself to feel
how your body responds to the apology and what emotions the
apology elicits. Allow it to begin to heal your wounds.

Learn to Accept an Apology

Taking in an apology—allowing it to heal your wounds—is one
thing; accepting it is another. When we *accept* an apology, it usually
follows that we are willing to forgive the person for the wrongdoing, even if we can't forgive him or her at the moment. In fact, for
most people, accepting an apology opens the door to forgiveness.
This is how an acquaintance explained it to me: "Once I've accepted
someone's apology, I am more open to forgiving them. It may take
some time, but at least there is a willingness on my part."

To not accept an apology is similar to refusing to accept a gift.
To refuse to accept an apology is a powerful statement. It often sig-
nals a significant change in the relationship and may even indicate

that the relationship is over. For some people, to accept an apology from a wrongdoer is actually repugnant, since they want nothing whatsoever to do with him or her. But for most of us, there is a recognition of the courage it took to apologize and a softening of the heart. As my friend, Sharon, shared with me:

> When someone apologizes to me, it opens my heart more than anything else can. I can't imagine not accepting someone's heartfelt apology, no matter how angry or hurt I feel. I accept for me and for them. I accept in order to clean up the relationship, even if I have no intention of continuing it. But for me, accepting an apology and forgiving are two different things. Accepting an apology opens my heart to the *potential* for forgiveness, but I have a difficult time trusting someone who has hurt me.

I think this is true for most people. While we may intuitively know that we should accept an apology as the gift that it is, it does not follow that we will necessarily be able to forgive the wrongdoer. And just because we are *willing* to forgive doesn't mean that we are necessarily *ready* to forgive. While our acceptance opens the door to forgiveness, it will likely take more work and more time before we can truly forgive. We may need time to assimilate the apology, to examine our emotions, and to discover whether we feel the person's words seemed sincere.

The Connection Between Apology, Compassion, and Empathy

In order to truly forgive, most people need to gain empathy and compassion for the wrongdoer. This is where apology comes in. When someone apologizes, it makes it a lot easier for us to view him or her in a compassionate way. Once we have been able to feel compassion for the person who offended us, we can gain empathy, which in turn makes it easier to forgive.

Let's look closer at how apology, compassion, and empathy work hand in hand. When someone hurts us, we can react in several ways. Initially, most people try to defend themselves, which often leads to resentment, a desire for revenge, and an attempt to avoid the offending person. But another option is to forgive, letting go of our resentment, anger, and spite, and feeling compassion for the person who hurt us. The defensive responses are somewhat automatic. Forgiveness takes effort.

Psychological research and anecdotal evidence show that when people apologize for something they have done to hurt us, we find it easier to forgive them. Think for a moment about what happens inside you when someone who has hurt you says, "I'm sorry for what I did. I didn't mean to hurt you." Most people find that something inside them softens, their anger dissipates, and they find that forgiveness comes easier.

When a wrongdoer confesses and apologizes for hurting us, we are then able to develop a new image of this person. Instead of seeing him or her through a lens of anger and bitterness, the person's humility and apology cause us to see him or her as a fallible, vulnerable human being instead of the embodiment of evil. We see the wrongdoer as more like us, and this moves us. And because the wrongdoer appears broken and contrite, we can begin to see that this person is in need of mercy, not revenge.

To Empathize Is to Forgive

Michael E. McCullough, Ph.D., Steven J. Sandage, M.S., and Everett L. Worthington Jr., Ph.D., examined whether the relationship between apology and our capacity to forgive is due to our increased empathy for an apologetic offender. They discovered that much of why people find it easier to forgive an apologetic wrongdoer is that apology and confession increase their empathy for their offenders, which changes their ability to forgive.

Dr. McCullough, director of research at the privately funded National Institute for Healthcare Research in Rockville, Maryland, believes that apology encourages forgiveness by eliciting sympathy. He and his colleagues recently published two studies in the *Journal of Personality and Social Psychology* that support this hypothesis.

The first study, of 131 female and 108 male college students, looked at whether people who forgave are more conciliatory toward, and less avoidant of, their offender. Participants filled out questionnaires describing an event in which someone had hurt them, how they were hurt, how wrong the offender was, and the extent to which the offender apologized.

McCullough and his colleagues then measured the degree of empathy that participants felt toward the offending person, the degree to which they'd forgiven the offender, the degree to which participants had tried to reconcile with the offender, and the degree to which participants avoided the offender.

The data supported their hypothesis that an apology leads to empathy, and empathy mediates forgiveness. People who forgave also were less spiteful and avoidant of the person who had hurt them.

In a second study, McCullough and his colleagues experimented with empathy and measured the effect on forgiveness. They solicited participants who wanted help forgiving someone who had hurt them and randomly assigned them to two seminars or put them on a waiting list control group.

One seminar promoted empathy as a precursor to forgiving, and the other encouraged forgiving but did not foster empathy. Seminars met for a total of 8 hours over 2 days. Participants in the empathy seminar reported more empathy for their offenders than participants in the nonempathy seminar or those on the waiting list. They were also more willing to forgive their offenders at the end of the weekend than participants in the nonempathy sessions or those on the waiting list.

The Connection Between Being Forgiven and Compassion

The more we are forgiven for our offenses, the more compassionate and forgiving we can become. While receiving an apology encourages us to feel more empathy toward our wrongdoers and more forgiving, it also follows that the more we are forgiven, the more likely we are to have compassion toward our wrongdoers and to forgive them.

When President Clinton was acquitted on charges of perjury and obstruction of justice, Sam Donaldson asked him, "In your heart, can you forgive and forget?" Clinton visibly flinched. His face seemed to redden with anger. But then he seemed to mellow. With a little more humility on his face, Clinton answered, "I believe that any person who asks for forgiveness has to be prepared to give it."

Other Benefits of Forgiveness

In addition to making us more compassionate, humane beings, forgiveness brings many other personal benefits:

- Forgiveness helps relieve some of the pain we felt due to the offense and helps the wound begin to heal.

- When you forgive, you take an important step toward mending and rebuilding the relationship between you and the wrongdoer.

- When you forgive, you remove a burden that has been weighing you down.

- Forgiveness helps you to go on with your life instead of holding onto the past.

- Forgiveness makes you a better person and improves your overall mental and emotional health.

The Proof Is In

Several studies have shown that remaining angry, obsessing about revenge, and constantly reliving a painful incident are physically and emotionally stressful, whereas forgiveness is healing to the body, mind, and spirit.

Over the past decade, Robert Enright, Ph.D., of the University of Wisconsin–Madison, has investigated the nature of forgiveness. He and other researchers have found that those who forgive someone who has hurt them seem to reap significant mental health benefits. And according to studies of long-married couples, the act of forgiving appears to be one of the basic processes that keeps personal relationships functioning.

Research also shows that forgiveness can be liberating. Carrying around a desire for revenge or a need to avoid someone is not healthy. Hostility and aggression are linked to a host of health problems. Research by Enright and colleagues consistently finds that people who are able to forgive benefit through a decrease in anxiety, depression, and hostility, and an increase in hope, self-esteem, and existential well-being.

Although most experts agree that forgiveness is the healthiest thing to do, it is not always possible, at least not right away. By learning to receive and accept an apology, you are opening the door to the possibility of forgiveness. Whether you choose to walk through that door is up to you.

While forgiveness is a process that often takes time, for many people all the time in the world won't help them. Some feel that no apology can undo the damage that has been done and that the wrongdoer did something so horrible that forgiveness is impossible. Others feel that more than an apology is in order—that the wrong-doer needs to make restitution of some kind. Still others don't trust the apology; they fear that the wrongdoer is just trying to get back on their good side or manipulate them into forgiving so that this person can turn around and hurt them again.

In some cases, these feelings may be warranted, and the best you can do is accept someone's apology and move on, closing the door to any possibility of a continued relationship or reunion. But in other situations, these feelings may be smokescreens hiding the real reason for your inability to forgive—obstacles that not only prevent you from forgiving but from moving past the pain and getting on with your life. In the next chapter, we will explore these obstacles in depth, as well as ways to overcome them.

CHAPTER 6

Overcoming the Seven Obstacles to Forgiveness

Revenge has no more quenching effect on emotions than salt water has on thirst.

WALTER WECKLER

I imagine one of the reasons people cling to their hates so stubbornly is because they sense, once hate is gone, they will be forced to deal with pain.

JAMES BALDWIN

Forgiveness is the act of admitting we are like other people.

CHRISTINA BALDWIN

THE POWER OF APOLOGY PRINCIPLE 6

When we judge other people, we are putting ourselves in a position above them; when we have empathy, we put ourselves in their place.

In this chapter we explore the major obstacles to forgiveness: anger, fear, pride, black-and-white thinking, unreasonable expectations, judgment, and lack of empathy. Equally important, in Chapter 7 we discuss when it is best to try to work past our resistance to forgiveness and when it is best to honor it.

Obstacle 1: Anger

Often an apology will help melt the heart of the person who is angry. If an apology is sincere and the offending party is genuinely sorry for what he or she has done, many have been surprised to find their anger dissolving right on the spot. This is especially true when the action was unintentional, for example, someone inadvertently saying something that hurt your feelings or accidentally breaking something you love. Even in some of the most extreme cases involving murder, brutality, or rape, people have been able to forgive when a genuine apology was forthcoming.

But even the sincerest of apologies doesn't always help some people move toward forgiveness. Their hearts have been so hardened by hate that no apology can suffice, no matter how well meaning.

Many people don't want to give up their feelings of anger in order to forgive. For many it is their anger that helps them get through even the most difficult and painful situations. If someone harms us or someone we love, our anger can help us hold up against the pain. For example, in cases where a loved one is injured or killed at the hands of someone else, it is often feelings of anger, revenge, or the determination to achieve justice that helps a family survive the loss. If they were to let go of the anger, they would be left with the feelings of loss, which seem unbearable.

For these people, an apology may seem useless. They reason that nothing will help them but seeing the person who harmed their loved one punished or dead. Their hatred and rage have given them something to live for, and they don't want it taken away. Nothing— not an apology, not an acknowledgment of the pain caused, not restitution—will help them to move toward forgiveness.

I don't believe anger is a negative emotion. Anger is very powerful and can be used in many positive ways—to motivate us toward change, to strengthen us against our adversaries, and to protect us against pain. But sometimes we get stuck in our anger and are unable to move past it.

Revenge Isn't So Sweet

One of the ways we stay stuck in our anger is by constantly entertaining thoughts of revenge. Often those who desperately cling to their anger advocate the firmest punishment or the ultimate punishment—death. But even if their revenge fantasies were to come true, they wouldn't have the kind of peace that only forgiveness can bring.

Some people do more than fantasize about revenge. They actively seek it. The woman who slept with other men to get back at her husband for being unfaithful, the man who beat up the person who jilted his daughter, the woman who was determined to take her husband for all his money in a divorce proceeding, the man who decided to ruin his ex–business partner for leaving the firm—they all learned that although revenge certainly can temporarily be sweet, in time it becomes clear that no amount of revenge can heal the wounds caused by another's betrayal, carelessness, or rejection. Only by being willing to work past the anger and face the pain underneath can we begin to soothe our wounds. And only by being willing to ask for and accept an apology and then move toward forgiveness will our wounds be healed.

Having an affair to get back at an unfaithful partner doesn't take away the pain of your partner's betrayal, spreading lies about the person who ruined your reputation won't help you resurrect your public image, and destroying the property of the lover who dumped you won't take away the pain you feel from being abandoned. It's important to see revenge as the illusion that it is. We can never avenge a wrong. Constantly nursing your wounds and fantasizing about revenge keeps you negatively connected to the wrongdoer and unable to go on with your life. If you want to truly break free from a relationship, you need to release your anger in more constructive ways.

As long as you continue to have thoughts of revenge, you deplete your energy, which can be better spent in more positive ways, such as thinking of how to improve your life or working on understanding why you are attracted to people who hurt or betray you.

Many people have been known to get sick both physically and emotionally from harboring revenge and hatred. It just isn't worth it. If everyone were punished in kind for all their wrongdoings, we would all be in bad shape. Think of some of the mistakes, transgressions, and offenses you have committed in your life and imagine what your life would be like if everyone you wronged exacted revenge on you.

Getting to the Pain Underneath the Anger

One of the main reasons we hold onto our anger for dear life is that as long as we stay angry we don't have to feel the pain hiding underneath. Because anger can feel empowering, it may feel better to hold onto it rather than to feel vulnerable. But unless we face our pain, we are never going to be able to get past the experience of being hurt or betrayed and we will stay stuck in anger and stuck in the past, as was the case with Janette:

> I stayed angry with my mother for over 10 years. My hatred toward her is what kept me going. As long as I was angry with her for not protecting me from my stepfather, I didn't have to face the pain of her betrayal. It was just more than I could take at the time.
>
> But through the years I began to recognize that my anger wasn't subsiding. And while my anger made me feel powerful for a while, after a few years it began to sap my energy. I began to get sick a lot, and depressed. During one of my illnesses, I finally faced some of the pain I'd been pushing down for years. I know being in therapy helped. I couldn't feel it all at once—it was just too much. But gradually I let myself feel a little at a time.
>
> I'd faced the *fact*, the *concept* that my mother had allowed my stepfather to sexually abuse me, but I hadn't faced it *emotionally*. Once I started letting myself do that, things really started happening. I was in a great deal of pain, but I was also able to begin moving through the pain and through the betrayal. Since I hadn't let myself really feel what had happened, I hadn't been able to move past it. My anger and avoidance had kept me right in the middle of it.
>
> It took a while to process all the pain, but finally I was through it. And I was now willing to face my mother with it. Before all this, I couldn't stand to see her, and each time I did see her, I'd become enraged all over again. There seemed to be no end to it. But now when I saw her, I felt the pain—the overwhelming pain.

She noticed the difference right away. Instead of becoming defensive, the way she had for so long, she looked genuinely concerned. "What's wrong with you?" she asked me. "What happened?"

Now that I wasn't overtaken by my anger, I could actually speak to her. "I'm finally facing the pain of what happened to me," I explained.

"It seems to me you've been facing it for a long time," she said sarcastically.

"No, Mom, I wasn't. I was just feeling the anger. I was afraid to feel the pain."

She started to put up a wall, but then she looked more closely at me and I guess she realized that I wasn't going to attack her. "Well, I'm sorry to see you in pain, but it's good to see you when you're not angry."

"Yeah, I'll bet it is. It feels good to me too—not to be so angry with you, that is."

And then we actually smiled at each other. That may not seem to be such a big deal, but we hadn't smiled at each other in over 10 years, ever since I had my memories come up. We still have a long way to go, but now I feel hopeful. I can actually see a time when I might be able to forgive her.

Janette and her mother still have a lot of talking to do. The next step is for Janette to find out if her mother is willing to listen to her pain. But at least there's an opening there, whereas before the door was completely shut by her anger.

EXERCISE
Release Your Anger

Many people try to forgive before they have given themselves a chance to process their feelings, particularly their anger. *If you try to forgive before releasing your anger, your attempts will be fruitless.* As long as you are still angry, you can't forgive because the anger will overpower your feelings of forgiveness.

A. Write down all the reasons why you are angry with the person in question. Writing helps us get in touch with our true feelings. It brings emotions to the surface that have been buried deep inside us—emotions we have been afraid to acknowledge. Writing down your feelings helps with the confusion you often feel about why you are angry.

B. Now write a letter to the person who wronged you, outlining all the reasons why you are angry and hurt. Don't censor yourself; say exactly what you feel. Explain in detail how the person's actions or inaction harmed you. You can decide at a later date whether you wish to actually send the letter. For now, the purpose of the letter is to help you get your anger and pain out.

Obstacle 2: Fear

Some people refuse to think about an incident that caused them great pain, much less to focus on forgiving those who caused it. They are afraid that remembering will reopen old wounds and cause them to feel the pain all over again.

Another fear that prevents people from forgiving is that if they trust again, they will be hurt again. Many of those who have difficulty forgiving have been hurt a great deal in their life and therefore have serious trust issues. If your childhood was marked by neglect or abuse, particularly if it came at the hands of someone who was supposed to love and care for you, you probably find it difficult to trust others. If, as a child, you found you couldn't trust those closest to you, how are you supposed to be able to trust anyone?

The same holds true for those who have been deeply hurt as adults, including those who have been betrayed by a lover, those who have suffered from emotional or physical abuse at the hands of a mate, victims of rape, and those who were the victims of sexual abuse or sexual harassment by a teacher, boss, therapist, or doctor. If you experienced any of these things, not only will you find it difficult to forgive the offender but to trust new people who come into your life. If love and trust have become synonymous with pain, how are you supposed to be able to open your heart to anyone again?

If you have experienced any of these events and then have been hurt by a friend, co-worker, or new lover, you may decide that it simply isn't worth being in the relationship any longer. It may have taken all the courage you could muster to enter the relationship in the first place, and it may have taken months or even years to build up enough trust in the other person to allow yourself to take down the protective walls and begin to get close. Even the smallest transgression on the part of another person—one harsh word, one lie, one missed date—can catapult you back behind your wall of safety and make it difficult for you to peek around it again, much less take it down. If the transgression is a more serious one—such as breaking a confidence, becoming angry and saying hurtful things, or in the case of a romantic relationship, flirting or being unfaithful—it may feel impossible for you to forgive.

Obstacle 3: Pride

Just as pride can get in the way of being willing to apologize, it can also be an obstacle to taking in an apology and forgiving. Some people are too proud to admit they have even been hurt, since to them admitting hurt is admitting weakness or vulnerability. Others are so insulted when someone wrongs them that they feel accepting an apology is tantamount to giving up their pride.

Pride can prevent us from facing our own faults and weaknesses. If we make the other person all bad, we don't have to face our part in the interaction or any of our own shortcomings that might have contributed to the problem. Holding onto unforgiveness becomes a protective defense against self-examination.

Obstacle 4: Black-and-White Thinking

Some people live by the motto "If you hurt me once, you are a fool; if you hurt me twice, I am the fool." They firmly believe that it is foolish to believe that a person can change, and that once someone has hurt you, you can't trust that person. Therefore, no matter how sincere the apology or how well intentioned a wrongdoer is, they never entirely forgive. These people are caught up in black-and-white thinking. To them a person is either good or bad—there are no gray areas, no second chances.

When we think in this way, we make it nearly impossible to forgive, no matter how many apologies we receive. The person who hurt us automatically becomes all bad and we find it difficult to see anything good about him or her from that time forward.

Those who have black-and-white thinking tend to put others on pedestals at the beginning of a relationship. They find someone they can admire, someone who appears to embody their image of perfection and they place too much adoration and trust in that person. Then, when he or she makes a mistake, which will inevitably happen, they are deeply disappointed. They knock the other person off the pedestal and see him or her as all bad.

Get Past Your Black-and-White Thinking

Most of us tend to feel more comfortable when things seem clear-cut—good or bad, black or white. Ambiguity—the gray areas that characterize most of real life—makes us feel uncomfortable and unsettled. But no one is all good or all bad. We all have good and bad qualities; we all share the capacity to do both good and evil.

The psychological defense mechanism known as *splitting* causes us to divide thoughts, emotions, and behaviors into two mutually exclusive categories—good or bad, black or white—making ourselves and others either perfect or failures, saints or sinners.

Becoming more forgiving of others and ourselves requires acceptance of the range of grays that make us human. We are each a composite, a mosaic of different thoughts, emotions, and choices of behavior. And we are each more developed and mature in some areas than in others. For example, a person can be well intentioned yet lack social skills; someone may be extremely magnanimous when it comes to helping the needy yet be afraid of true intimacy with his or her partner. Rather than thinking in terms of *good* and *bad*, we must begin to think in terms of developed and undeveloped, aware and unaware. The more aware we are, the further along we are on our emotional and spiritual path.

If we require perfection in others, we miss out on great friends and great teachers. It is possible for a person to be a great leader and at the same time have many faults. It is possible for someone to be unfaithful in his or her marriage and still be a good person. And it is possible to be a wonderful parent *and* be impatient, to be kind *and* selfish, to be loving *and* occasionally judgmental, to be a nice person *and* angry at the same time. And no matter who we are and how hard we have worked to become whole and aware, we will still make mistakes. We need to accept our humanity and that of others with all its imperfections.

In rejecting the tyranny of black-and-white thinking, we become less rigid, self-righteous, stuffy, and judgmental and more flexible, accepting, spontaneous, and loving.

Obstacle 5: Having Unreasonable Expectations of Others

When our expectations of others are too high, we are continuously disappointed. In order to forgive, we must understand that we all make mistakes, we all fall short of our potential, and we all have a dark side.

Most of us are far too critical of others, far too impatient with our partners, our children, and our co-workers or employees. We lack the compassion and empathy necessary to understand that most people are doing the best they can under their present circumstances. Sure, most partners could be more considerate and loving, most children could do better in school and respect their parents more, and most employees could do a better job, but we never know what internal conflicts or external problems might be affecting their personality or performance. Instead of remembering this, we tend to be impatient and become angry when our expectations are not met. And instead of letting the other person know how we feel and asking for an apology, we often become critical and judgmental and distance ourselves from the other person.

Obstacle 6: Sitting in Judgment

Perhaps the biggest obstacle to forgiveness is our tendency to judge others harshly. Being able to quickly get past the inevitable hurts and disappointments we will experience at the hands of others is a sign of maturity. So is getting past our tendency to be self-righteous. As one client, a mature woman of 53, told me:

> When I was younger, I found it difficult to forgive anybody for anything. I was extremely self-righteous. But that was before I experienced my own fall from grace and came to realize that I was no better than many of the people I had judged so harshly. Nowadays, when someone makes a mistake or

hurts my feelings, I usually say, "That's okay. Nobody's perfect—including me!"

My Story

For most of my life I was one of the most judgmental people you could hope to meet. I came by it honestly. I was raised by people who were experts on any given subject, who were the first to state their opinion, to give advice, and to tell everyone and anyone what they should do to change. Their advice was always gospel, their opinion always right.

I was so judged and criticized growing up that I learned to become an expert at it myself. I learned to judge others before they had a chance to judge me. Unfortunately, it is a fact of life that those of us who were judged as children (and as adults) are the most likely to judge others.

I became the expert, the authority, the person who looked down her nose pompously at other people. I was wiser, more capable, more "right" than anyone I knew. Few people argued with me, and those who did had a major fight on their hands. I was a natural litigator, and several people told me I should have become a lawyer.

I believe we were all put on this earth to learn certain lessons and we are constantly being presented with opportunities to learn our lessons. When we don't learn our lesson in one situation, we can be assured that we will be presented with another opportunity to learn it—and another, and another.

It takes a lifetime (and some believe several lifetimes) to learn our lessons. It takes all our time and energy and focus. No one else can teach us our lessons. We must learn them on our own, in our own time, through our own struggles. By the same token, we can't teach anyone else *their* lessons, which is what judgment is all about.

I believe that one of the most important lessons we are all learning is to be less judgmental of others. It certainly has been one of my strongest lessons. I have been blessed by being forced to learn this and it has changed my life. But I haven't learned it easily. In fact, it has been a difficult and painful lesson, one that has often felt as if it were thrust upon me without my consent.

Throughout the years, this lesson has gradually been intensifying, although looking back on my life, I realize it has always been a driving force. Eventually I realized that *each* and *every* time I judge another person negatively, I soon find myself in that person's shoes, experiencing the same things, fully able to understand his or her perspective.

For a long time, I resented this experience. While I took note of it, I didn't see the positive power in it, only the irony and the pain. It felt to me as if I were constantly having my nose rubbed in my own shit. And like a defiant dog, I didn't learn my lesson—I just became more stubborn.

It wasn't until about 7 years ago that I finally saw the blessing in my dilemma. I was being forced to learn to be empathetic in a most profound way. And for someone as stubborn, self-centered, and judgmental as myself, it took force for me to learn.

For many years, I was extremely judgmental of my mother for being so narcissistic and emotionally abusive. I also found myself being critical of many of my clients' parents who had been neglectful or abusive. But as I slowly faced my own narcissism and abusiveness, I found it harder and harder to judge others. I knew how hard it was for me to finally acknowledge my own faults and shortcomings, and for the first time I came to realize how very difficult it is for all of us to admit our problems, especially when we discover how much we may have damaged someone else. I learned just how humiliating it is to own up to negative behavior if you've always seen yourself as a victim or someone who really cares about people.

From that time forward, I have been continually forced to face my tendency to judge. Here is one simple example: I was driving down the road when I found myself behind a slow driver. I immediately became impatient and started fuming about how this person was holding me up, cursing at her for driving so slow and inconveniencing *me*. I ended up passing the slower car, cursing all the while about how slow the person was driving. Then within minutes I was on my merry way and had put aside the experience.

But only a few days later, I was forced to eat my words, forced to regret having judged that poor driver so harshly. My car had suddenly lost power as I was going up a steep hill. I had my foot all the way down on the gas, but my car was just crawling up the hill. I wasn't even sure I was going to make it. Suddenly I heard a car honking behind me. I looked up to see a man in a car riding my tail, honking and swearing at me for driving so slow. I looked in my rear-view mirror and mouthed the words, "I can't help it. My car won't go any faster."

In that moment I had an "Aha" experience. I thought to myself, *My God, that's what I was like. That poor slow driver. She probably had a good reason for driving slowly. How dare I be so belligerent and impatient? After all, I don't own the road.*

My lesson learned, from that time on I have been much more patient with slow drivers. When I start to get impatient, I am immediately reminded of my insight.

We've all had experiences like this. We've all been on both sides of a situation as the slow driver and the fast driver. And many of you may have seen the irony as I did. But how many of you saw it as a lesson? We are all judgmental. The point is to become *aware* of judging and to make it our intention to be as nonjudgmental as humanly possible.

EXERCISE
Discover Why You May Be Stuck in Judgment

The following exercises may help you discover why you may be stuck in judgment:

A. Ask yourself, "What do I get out of being judgmental or critical?" Write your answers down on a piece of paper.

B. If you find you are stuck for answers, the following possibilities may give you some ideas. If you'd like, you can use them as a checklist. I judge other people because:

- It makes me feel in control.
- It keeps me separate from others.
- It is a way of protecting myself from pain.
- It is a way of protecting myself from intimacy.
- It is a way of feeling superior.
- It helps me hide my feelings of insecurity.
- It is a habit.
- It makes me feel powerful.

C. Notice under what conditions you tend to be the most judgmental. The next time you catch yourself feeling judgmental, ask yourself the following questions:

1. What emotions am I feeling?

2. How am I feeling physically?

3. How secure am I feeling? Am I feeling threatened? Criticized? Rejected?

4. Are there times or circumstances when I tend to be more critical or judgmental than at other times?

5. What patterns do I notice (for example, do I tend to be more judgmental or critical when I am feeling tired, hurt, threatened, angry)?

D. Pay attention to how you behave with different people and ask yourself the following questions:

1. Do I tend to be more judgmental/critical of some people than others?

2. Do I tend to be more judgmental when I am around certain people? For example, when I am with my old friends from school? Or when I am around judgmental people?

Choose Empathy Over Judgment

We tend to be critical and judgmental of others because we lack empathy for their position. When we judge other people we are, in essence, putting ourselves in a position *above* them. In contrast, *when we have empathy we put ourselves in their place. Judging is a position of superiority; empathy is a position of equality.*

Now that you have a better understanding of the reasons why you judge, the next step to overcoming your tendency to judge others is to make a conscious decision to choose empathy over judgment (lack of empathy is the next obstacle to be discussed). Once this decision has been made, you are on your way.

Not only does choosing empathy over judgment help us to forgive, but it helps us become fuller, deeper, more compassionate human beings. Here are some of the personal benefits of empathy:

1. Judging makes us pompous, self-righteous, hard-hearted. Empathy softens us and makes us more open-hearted and wise. Judging causes us to contract, to become small and narrow-minded. Empathy causes us to expand into more open-minded people.

2. Judging blinds us to others. Empathy helps us to see others far more clearly—both their positive and negative qualities. It is like a magic telescope that helps us to see inside others, to view their heart and soul.

3. Judging separates us from others, whereas empathy connects us and helps us to see our similarities, joining us in our humanity.

4. It is important to realize that our relationship with others mirrors our relationship with ourselves. The way we treat others is the way we treat ourselves, and vice versa. If we judge others, we judge ourselves, and if we judge ourselves, we judge others. The Bible makes clear this connection in the famous line: "Do unto others as you would have others do unto you."

The suspension of judgment in no way implies the suspension of discrimination. These are completely different functions. In forgiving a murderer by being compassionate and understanding the roots of his actions, for example, we don't let him out of jail unless he is rehabilitated. In forgiving a friend who hurt our feelings, we are not required to overlook her action but to communicate our feelings of hurt and anger to her.

The following information will help you to move from your self-righteous position of judgment to one of compassion and empathy. Although you may at first feel resistant to this information, deep in your heart you will recognize the inherent truth in it. Allow yourself to face these truths, for your own sake and for those who need forgiving.

- *To judge is to misjudge.* No one truly knows another person, their intentions, or their motivations. And no matter how a person "acts" in public, no one knows how he or she really feels about what he or she has done.

  When we judge someone, we presume to know him and to know his motivations. Since we can never really know another person, to judge means to misjudge.

- *Judging is taking the focus off ourselves.* Pay attention to what happens when you are upset with someone, when you feel angry or judgmental about what someone else is doing. Notice how often you think about the other person, obsess about his behavior, focus on how he should change, or concentrate on what you'd like to say to him about his behavior. Notice how much time and energy you spend focusing away from yourself and your own issues.

  Judging others is a trap. It is an easy, convenient way to avoid ourselves and our own lessons. It depletes us of our energy—energy that could be better spent focusing on improving ourselves.

We lose ourselves when we are busy judging someone else. Our energy is drawn outward instead of inward where it belongs. We stop learning about ourselves and stop focusing on our own lessons when we get caught up in trying to teach someone else.

- *Judging others causes us to lie and to blind ourselves to the truth.* When we judge others, we are choosing to ignore the fact that either (1) we have done the same thing, (2) we have thought of doing the same thing, or (3) we have come close to doing the same thing.

Whenever you find yourself judging someone else or you are having a difficult time forgiving someone, read over the above list. It may help remind you of why you are judging and why it is important to stop.

Finally, I'd like to share with you an important dream I had concerning judgment. In the dream I was watching people with a critical eye, noticing how much they were envying one another, judging one another, putting one another down. A wise spiritual guide said to me, "Now look at them and see their hearts." I did this, visualizing a red heart inside of each person. Then my guide said, "Now imagine that each and every one of them is saying, 'Please accept me. Please love me.'" I did this, and suddenly all my judgments were gone. I saw them for who they really were—people who wanted to be loved and accepted just like me.

This dream was extremely vivid and it stayed with me for several days afterward. I knew instantly it was important and I knew it had come to me as a great lesson. Whenever I begin to judge someone, I remember the dream and follow the words of my guide. I look into the other person's heart and see past his or her anger, pettiness, selfishness, or resistance to who the person really is. I hope the dream helps you as well.

Obstacle 7: Lack of Empathy

In order for some of us to gain empathy for wrongdoers, we need to admit to ourselves that we have been guilty of committing the same or a similar offense. It is easier to judge others than to remind ourselves that we, too, are capable of such acts, that we, too, are fallible, vulnerable human beings with rage, lust, fear, greed, and envy in our hearts, that "there but for the grace of God, go I." All of us are capable of committing selfish or cruel acts—a fact that most of us fail to accept. We are all capable of lying, stealing, cheating, having fantasies of wanting to kill someone. Negative emotions and traits—rage, jealousy, shame, resentment, lust, greed, suicidal and murderous tendencies—lie concealed just beneath the surface, masked by our more proper selves. These repressed and denied emotions and traits are what psychologists call our Shadow or dark side. Those who are familiar with their Shadow will be less judgmental and more empathetic of others. Conversely, those who will not or cannot admit to their own human frailties are the most judgmental of the frailties of others.

Own Your Projections

Projection is the act of attributing to others those feelings and reactions that we ourselves are having but do not want to acknowledge, or in some cases, feelings that we fear we may now have or have had in the past. Just as a movie camera projects an image onto a screen, we project our own image onto other people. Others aren't blank screens, of course. They have their own faults, prejudices, and judgments. But much of what we are perceiving when we judge or criticize another person is a projection of our own image.

Because projection is an unconscious defense mechanism, we are not necessarily aware of it. In fact, more times than not, we are unaware of it. Projection kicks in whenever an unrecognized trait or characteristic of our personality becomes activated. As a result of the unconscious projection, we observe and react to this unrecognized personal trait in other people. We see in them something that is a part of ourselves, even though we fail to see it in ourselves.

By understanding projection, we can come to understand that our judgments of others have much more to do with ourselves than with those we judge. Therefore, those we are critical or judgmental of can be our best teachers, since they expose parts of ourselves that we have rejected, denied, or hidden.

EXERCISE
Become Aware of Your Personal Projections

A. List all the qualities you do not like in other people, for instance, conceit, short temper, selfishness, bad manners, greed, and others.

B. When the list is finally complete (and it will probably be quite lengthy), highlight those characteristics that you not only dislike in others but hate, loathe, and despise. This shorter list will be a fairly accurate picture of your Shadow projections. For example, if you list arrogance as a trait in others that you simply cannot stand and if you tend to be highly critical of those who are arrogant, you would do well to examine your own behavior to see if perhaps you, too, practice arrogance.

Of course, not all criticisms of others are projections of your own undesirable traits. But any time your response to another person involves excessive emotions or overreaction, you can be sure that something within you is being activated. While there may be a certain degree of reasonableness about your offense at a person's behavior, in true projection your condemnation will far exceed the person's demonstration of the fault.

Put Yourself in the Other Person's Place

In addition to acknowledging that you are capable of or have committed the same mistakes, errors in judgment, or offenses as others and taking back your projections, you can learn to be more empathetic by imagining you are in the other person's place, seeing things from his or her perspective. The following exercises will help you with this process.

EXERCISE
Practice Being Empathetic

A. Think of someone with whom you are having difficulties. Write about the situation. Describe the conflict from the perspective of the other person. For example, let's say that you and your brother are always fighting because he doesn't help out more with your aging mother. You've been left to carry the burden and you think he's a selfish, inconsiderate brother and son. This is how you might do the exercise:

"I am Lily's brother. Lily is always criticizing me for the way I live my life. She thinks I should help out our mother more instead of always partying. I realize that she's carrying most of the burden, but she's older and more established. I think she's just jealous that I'm still young and not tied down to a job and marriage the way she is. Maybe if she'd get off my back I might feel more like helping out, but I resent her telling me what to do. After all, she is my sister, not my mother."

You might be surprised at the insights you gain from doing such an exercise. There really are two sides to a story and we need to be reminded of this, especially when we are locked into a conflict.

B. Imagine how a loved one might describe you to another person. Imagine you are a fly on the wall while your mate, child, or friend talks about you and your relationship with him or her.

⚶

How Empathy Can Help You to Forgive Even When There Is No Apology

Often those who have offended us are unwilling or unable to apologize. And sometimes the wrongdoer has died. How do we gain the necessary empathy in order to forgive under such circumstances? We can gain compassion and empathy for a wrongdoer when we come to admit to ourselves that we have all harmed other people, that we may be guilty of the same or similar acts as those that have been done to us. This realization can help us to forgive even when an apology is not forthcoming.

Another way is to attempt to see things from the other person's point of view and empathetically feel for that person. The following exercise will help you in this endeavor.

EXERCISE

Write About the Situation from the Wrongdoer's Perspective

A. Write a letter to the wrongdoer (even if he or she is dead) in which you confront him or her about the offense, how much it hurt or harmed you, and how you feel about what he or she did to you.

B. Now write from the perspective of the wrongdoer.

My client, Ariana, imagined how her father (who had died) might have responded to her angry letter from this exercise:

At first he made up excuses for his actions. Through me, he seemed to write:

I didn't know better.

I didn't know about any psychological consequences.

I didn't know my behavior would stop you from trusting men for the rest of your life.

I thought it was important to go to the doctor with you when your breasts grew differently.

I wanted you to get on in life.

I punished you to shut you up. I needed some peace and quiet after being out to work for 12 hours.

I know this all sounds like excuses, but this is my side of it!

I was not aware of any sexual energy between us. I was trying to be a proper parent. I'm sorry I hurt you beyond the actual punishment. I guess I did it all wrong—like most of everything in my life. I always fail. Life owes me—growing up without a father to look up to, brought up by mother and sister (women! . . .), wasted my youth in the war and prisoner-of-war camps, then I came back, married your mother (of all women! . . .), started work, and never stopped working; I never had any time for myself, coming home from work, whining children (all girls!); they were not very healthy and no good at school—and a woman complaining about them (also she couldn't stand living with me and was drinking). The companies I tried running all went bankrupt. I was just so angry!

I needed something to be proud of, something to make me feel worthy—but nothing worked. So I tried to keep everything and everybody in place. I hurt you, physically and emotionally, to make you behave the way I wanted you to. I hit rather than being unfaithful, to show her I do what I want. I hit the dog. . . . I spent a lot of time in clubs, etc., because there people liked me—they only saw my social side, open and cheerful, outgoing.

It was all-out stress. I got sicker and sicker. I had 2 years to live. Now let me rest in peace—I stopped living because I had enough of it!

Ariana was overwhelmed by what she had written. She'd never realized (at least consciously) what her father had been going through, why he treated her the way he did, or what he was thinking or feeling at any given time. This exercise seemed to give her insight into her father's life in a way that nothing else had. She hadn't received the apology she'd wanted from him, but she said she gained more of an understanding of her father and closure to the relationship.

No matter how you look at it, forgiveness is an act of love. It is a willingness to give—thus the word *forgive*—for-to-give. When we forgive, we help the person who wronged us to move past his or her shame and to have a new start in life. When we forgive, we inspire others, including the wrongdoer, to be more forgiving.

The only way to get to this state of love or willingness to give is to feel compassion and empathy for the wrongdoer. It is never too late to learn empathy or to increase your ability to empathize with others. By practicing and honing your empathy skills, you can move away from judgment and toward forgiveness.

EXERCISE

What Are Your Obstacles to Forgiveness?

After reading about the seven most common obstacles that prevent us from forgiving, you have probably gained more understanding about why you are having difficulties. The following exercise will help you still further:

A. Which of the seven obstacles to forgiveness do you feel is your biggest hurdle at this point in time? Write about this obstacle, why you feel you are still struggling with it, and how you plan on overcoming it.

B. Which of the seven obstacles have you worked through? Write about how you feel about having overcome them and how you did so. Reminding yourself of how far you've come will encourage you to do the necessary work to overcome those obstacles that still stand in your way.

True Forgiveness Often Requires an Emotional or Spiritual Transformation

Those who are truly able to forgive have usually gained a deep understanding of the concepts we discussed in this and the previous chapters (e.g., they have learned the importance of having compassion and empathy for others and of not judging others). But in order for these concepts to really sink in, many people must experience an emotional or spiritual transformation.

Often it takes a tragedy or near tragedy for us to come to a place of clarity about forgiveness. Survivors of plane crashes have often reported that during the minutes just prior to the crash they experienced an epiphany in which they either came to realize that truly loving others means being understanding and forgiving, or that life is too short to allow fights and arguments to become important.

Other times, it is when we begin to age or when we experience a life-threatening illness that we realize how important relationships are and how unimportant our hurt feelings or our petty differences are in the grand scheme of things. We see just how precious time is. We come to realize that life is too short to allow quarrels and misunderstandings to continue year after year.

Finally, sometimes it takes a "fall from grace" in order for us to gain the necessary empathy and compassion toward others. As I wrote in my book, *Blessings from the Fall*, there are few experiences in life as demoralizing, humiliating, and painful as falling from grace. For some, falling from grace is the horrible, shame-inducing experience of being publicly chastised or humiliated, having their reputation ruined and their good name irretrievably damaged, and being robbed of their dignity. For others, it is falling off their pedestal after years of being admired, adored, and emulated, or losing all they've worked for years to achieve—their financial status, their reputation, their very livelihood.

One of the many blessings that can come from such a fall from grace is that we learn to be more compassionate and empathetic toward others, and are thus more able to forgive others their mistakes, transgressions, and weaknesses. This was the case with Reverend Thomas Healy, who shared his story with me:

> Before my fall I was a pompous, judgmental person. I felt I was better than most people and was especially critical of those who sinned. Being a minister puts you in a position of power. People look up to you, and before long you begin to believe that you are better than others. But one of the many blessings I experienced as a result of my fall was that I came to realize that I am no better or worse than anyone else and that I have no right to judge anyone. I came to truly understand what Jesus meant by, "Let he who is without sin cast the first stone."

Forgiveness is an exercise in compassion and is both a process and an attitude. In the process of forgiveness, we transform the suffering created as a result of being hurt by others into psychological and spiritual growth. Through the attitude of forgiveness, we attain serenity by letting go of the ego's incessant need to judge ourselves and others.

Forgiveness is not a self-righteous or Polyanna-like turning of the other cheek or a condoning of abhorrent behavior. Neither is it forgetting. Forgiving requires us to acknowledge the other person's actions as harmful, but then to empathize with the other person. If we can understand the deep pain from which hurtful actions inflicted on us arose, then we have suffered with the other person; we have been compassionate. In that act of compassion, we move out of the role of victim and see beyond the actions to the heart of the wrongdoer.

CHAPTER 7

There Is a Time to Forgive—and a Time to Forget About Forgiving

God may forgive you, but I never can.

Elizabeth I
(to the Countess of Nottingham)

THE POWER OF APOLOGY PRINCIPLE 7

Each person needs to come to forgiveness on his or her own, and not be pressured to forgive because it is the politically correct thing to do.

Forgiveness is not an easy process, as you've learned in the previous chapter. Even those who intellectually understand the importance of forgiveness, even those who have a strong spiritual belief in forgiving, cannot achieve it unless they are willing to acknowledge and express their anger, feel their pain, and confront the other obstacles that stand in their way of forgiving.

Even so, there comes a time when it becomes clear that forgiveness is the most sensible, humane, and healthy thing to do. It's time to forgive when:

- The other person has given you a meaningful apology, but your pride or your stubbornness keeps rising up inside you telling you that he or she didn't apologize well enough or isn't sorry enough or didn't take enough of the blame.

- You know deep in your heart that the wrongdoer is truly sorry, whether or not he or she has had the courage to apologize.

- You know deep in your heart that you were both to blame.

- Your anger and stubbornness are causing you physical or emotional pain.

- Your anger and distrust are in the way of your loving and trusting others in your life.

- An estrangement is clearly hurting you more than it is the other person.

- Either you or the wrongdoer is getting old or is gravely ill, you love him or her, and you may not have much more time together.

Many people believe that forgiveness is necessary if we are to put the past behind us and move on. Twelve-step programs teach the philosophy that we should forgive others because they, like us, were doing the best they could at the time, and because they too were damaged by their upbringing. Many religions teach that forgiveness is the only fair and compassionate thing to do, since we have all sinned and we have all hurt others. Many psychotherapists also believe that forgiveness is necessary in order to gain healthy closure.

But as wise as spiritual leaders, philosophers, and therapists are concerning the importance of forgiveness, sometimes forgiveness is not possible. Unfortunately, because of the focus on forgiveness within the religious, 12-step, and even psychological communities, we have not been given permission to choose not to forgive. Contrary to popular belief, forgiveness is not necessary for healing, and in some cases forgiveness is not necessarily the healthiest thing to do. This is especially true when forgiving is tantamount to giving permission to hurt you again.

Sometimes Not Forgiving Can Be Healthy

Sometimes we need to hold onto the very thing that prevents us from forgiving in order to cope and survive. This is especially true with anger, a powerful motivator, especially empowering for those who have been victimized. Anger can help us rise above the victimization and fight our way back from the most devastating of traumas. This was Shelly's situation. When she was 8 years old, her father began sexually abusing her. The abuse continued throughout Shelly's childhood and even into her adolescence.

When I first began seeing Shelly, she was 22. She explained to me that at 16, she had finally been able to stand up to her father and stop him from continuing to molest her. His response had been to kick her out of the house (her mother no longer lived with them). Her father then proceeded to turn all of her relatives against her, telling them she had stolen from him. Shelly was forced to fend for herself with no help from anyone except a close friend.

For several years, Shelly tried to block out what her father had done to her in order to focus on surviving. But when she was 22, her life started crumbling around her and she knew she needed help. Shelly and I worked together for several years, in which time she was able to express a great deal of her anger toward her father. Her anger empowered her, and expressing it helped with her depression, which had been caused primarily by turning her anger toward her father inward on herself.

Then Shelly joined Alcoholics Anonymous. One of the ways she had blocked out her pain was to drink, and now that she was in therapy she began to recognize that drinking had become a problem. AA helped her with her compulsion to drink, and the support she received from fellow AA members felt like the only family she'd never had. But she became confused about the messages she was receiving from AA about the importance of forgiving her father.

Shelly had only seen her father briefly in all the years since she'd left home. He had supposedly "forgiven" her for "stealing" from him and had welcomed her back with open arms when she finally got up enough nerve to attend her cousin's wedding. At the wedding, her father, who had been drinking, started flirting with her, pressing his body up against her whenever he passed by her, and once even tried to grab her breast. This made her so uncomfortable that she left.

"How can I forgive my father when he denies molesting me?" she lamented during her next session. "And why should I forgive him when he's still doing the same thing he's always done? He hasn't changed a bit!"

It had been the emergence of her anger that had helped Shelly survive the trauma of her childhood. And it was anger that gave her the motivation to continue facing the pain and the feeling of betrayal that kept coming up as she worked toward recovery.

Clearly, Shelly wasn't ready to forgive—and she might never be. She needed her anger to help her feel separate from her father (victims of child sexual abuse often feel too enmeshed with their perpetrators, especially if it was a parent or sibling). She needed her anger to help ward off the overwhelming shame and guilt that constantly flooded over her (victims of all forms of childhood abuse, especially victims of sexual abuse, tend to blame themselves for the abuse). Shelley's anger was a constant reminder of how wrong her father was, and she needed that reminder when she began doubting herself (e.g., "Why didn't I stop him?").

There may come a time when Shelly no longer needs her anger. If this happens, she will be more able to look at forgiveness as a viable option. *But each person needs to come to this point on his or her own and not be pressured to forgive because it is the politically correct thing to do.* Although I have great respect for 12-step programs and know they continue to help millions of people, each person is unique and therefore needs to progress through the 12 steps at his or her own pace and in his or her own way. This includes deciding when and if they are able or willing to forgive.

When Sorry Isn't Good Enough

Sometimes our resistance to forgiving is telling us something important; instead of trying to get past our resistance, we need to honor it. Even though someone apologizes, it doesn't necessarily mean that we must forgive. For some people, there are situations that are truly unforgivable. For example, some offenses, such as murder or the sexual abuse of a child, are considered unforgivable by many. In other situations, such as when the person apologizing is a repeat offender, forgiving is impossible because there seems to be no hope for change.

This was the case with Megan. Shortly after she married, her husband began to physically abuse her. After every incident of abuse, he would begin to cry and plead with her to forgive him: "I'm sorry, Megan. Please forgive me. I didn't mean to. You just make me so mad. I promise I won't ever do it again."

Each time her husband apologized, Megan forgave him. Even though what he had done had devastated her, he seemed so pitiful and so sincere in his apologies that not forgiving him seemed like a heartless thing to do. She loved him dearly and wanted to believe he was genuinely sorry. But before long, he was punching her and pushing her around the room all over again.

It took 2 years before Megan finally came to the painful conclusion that her husband was never going to change. He'd promised to go to therapy many times, but each time had backed out at the last minute. And sometimes he'd manage to go months without abusing her, giving her the false hope that perhaps this time things really were going to be different. But after 2 years of this never-ending cycle, one day something changed inside Megan:

He came into our bedroom about an hour after beating me, looking sheepish, as usual. He proceeded to say he was sorry, that he didn't know what came over him, that he was going to get some help, that he loved me. But this time it just didn't work. I wasn't touched by the pain in his voice as I had always been in the past. And I wasn't moved by his apologies. I'd always believed that he really couldn't help himself and so I always believed he really was sorry. But suddenly I questioned his sincerity. It all sounded phony to me. I was shocked. It felt like I'd been fooled all this time. That he really wasn't sorry at all. That it was just words. Empty words. That was the day I decided I wasn't going to forgive him again. The time for forgiveness was over.

That night, while her husband was sleeping, Megan sneaked out of the house and never returned. That was a year ago. Since that time, Megan has managed to put her life back together and to resist the temptation to return to him, even though she often feels pulled in that direction.

The last time I saw Megan she told me, "It makes me so mad when people tell me I should forgive Max for what he did to me. They have no idea what forgiving him did to me all those years. And they don't understand that I can't afford to forgive him now. If I forgive him, I'm afraid I'll start to make excuses all over again for what he did to me. If I forgive him, I'm afraid I'll weaken and go back to him."

Perhaps with more time and distance, Megan will be able to

forgive her estranged husband. But for now she needs to keep her heart hardened against him. Who can blame her?

When Expecting Forgiveness Can Be an Insult

Sometimes expecting yourself or another person to forgive can actually be an insult. If you or a loved one had been a prisoner in one of the concentration camps of Nazi Germany, having to witness the horrendous deaths of your loved ones daily and personally suffering from the evil acts of torture, starvation, and humiliation at the hands of Hitler's henchmen, would you expect yourself to be able to forgive Hitler? Perhaps with a great deal of effort and spiritual focus you might be able to get to the place where you forgave the guards, recognizing that many were young men caught up in the fervor of the times or were even forced to serve. But do you believe you would be able to forgive Hitler himself? How about Timothy McVeigh? Before you become too judgmental about your own or someone else's inability to forgive, think about these situations and be honest with yourself about your responses.

Many survivors of the Holocaust will tell you that to forgive the atrocities of Hitler and the other Nazi leaders is to endorse or condone what they did. This is also how some survivors of violent crime and horrendous childhood abuse feel.

When Forgiveness Is Unhealthy

Forgiveness is supposed to be healing for everyone concerned. But in many cases forgiveness can actually be damaging—or rather false forgiveness can be damaging. When family members pressure one member into forgiving another in order to instill family harmony, they are in essence sacrificing that person for the supposed good of the entire family. This can be far too reminiscent of what happened when the victim was a child.

In response to my book, *Divorcing a Parent*, I received this letter:

My brother has never apologized for torturing me as a child. For nearly ten years I endured his constant domination and emotional and physical abuse almost daily. It seemed like from the moment I woke up until I went to bed he was on me—pushing me around, hitting me, wrestling me to the

ground and twisting my arms and legs, ordering me around.
Now my parents can't understand why I refuse to have a relationship with him. They think I should forgive and forget and
go on with my life. That I'm being silly and petty to hold onto
my anger after all these years.

But I've worked long and hard in therapy to come to a
place where I understand that I have a right to my anger—
toward my brother and my parents. After all, they allowed it
to go on for all those years; they turned their backs on what
he was doing and labeled it "roughhousing" and they're still
making excuses for his behavior today.

I'm not willing to have a relationship with my brother just
to please my parents. I've forgiven him for what he did to me
as a child. After all, he was a kid himself and was acting out
because our family was so screwed up. But I haven't forgiven
him for the way he's continued to treat me and others as an
adult. He doesn't push me around physically, but he tries to
emotionally. He still bullies everyone else around him. One
wife already left him because he battered her and I'm sure he's
doing the same thing to his present wife. Until he is man
enough to admit he has a problem and to go get some help,
I'm not willing to be around him and subject myself to his abusive behavior. And I'm not willing to participate in the denial
that permeates my family. How can I forgive something that
everyone in my family says doesn't even exist!

Denying one family member's pain and reality in order to protect another family member and create a pseudo-family harmony
puts undue pressure on the victim, which can actually be harmful to
him or her.

Often a family member's efforts to reunite other family members
is motivated not by concern for the victimized child's welfare but by
his or her own need for self-exoneration. This situation is then tantamount to emotionally abandoning the child all over again. Once
more, family members are putting their needs above the needs of the
child, or putting the needs of one child above those of the other.
This continuation of abandonment and betrayal can be extremely
harmful to the victim.

Pseudo-forgiveness also prevents other family members from

growing emotionally. The perpetrator of the offense needs to face up to what he or she did in order to begin the healing process. This person needs to acknowledge the act and the pain that ensued in order to remove the cloak of shame and guilt he or she no doubt carries around. And other family members need to face the truth about what occurred, including their own negligence in preventing or stopping the offense.

It is far more healing for a victim to receive the acknowledgment that a crime or abuse actually occurred than it is for an offender to receive pseudo-forgiveness from people who are still in denial as to what actually happened. The act of forgiveness should never negate a person's perceptions of reality. Nor should forgiveness feel like an excuse or condoning of an evil act. People have a right to hold offenders accountable for their behavior. And they have a right to an acknowledgment of the offense and to an apology or statement of remorse from the offender. To refuse people the right to these important things is like robbing them of their humanity.

If you haven't already done so, ask the person who offended you for an apology or an acknowledgment of the pain he or she caused. If the person refuses, you have a right to withhold forgiveness just as that person withheld an apology.

Spiritual Forgiveness Versus Human Forgiveness

You can forgive *spiritually*, however. There is a difference between forgiving a person directly—that is, agreeing to forgive the actual act—and forgiving him or her in your heart. You can come to a place of compassion and empathy, a place where you are no longer obsessed or driven by your anger and by the past, without letting the person off the hook for the offense.

Spiritual forgiveness is not the same as condoning or excusing unacceptable behavior. When I came to the place where I was able to forgive the man who sexually abused me as a child, I in no way excused his behavior. What he did to me was despicable and it caused me great harm. If I'd ever had the chance to confront him in person, I would have. Instead, I worked through my anger in therapy.

But getting past my anger didn't bring me that much closer to forgiveness. Because I worked with survivors of childhood abuse for so many years, hearing their stories of abuse only reinforced my resolve that childhood abuse, especially child sexual abuse, is an unforgivable act.

Therefore, I didn't work on forgiving this man and didn't feel any real motivation to do so. It took another miracle for me to be able to forgive him. It began when I gained more compassion and empathy for those who abused others through the revelation that I had also been abusive and had also caused harm to others. Then, through a series of spiritual experiences, including insights gained through a psychological method known as EMDR, I came to the life-changing awareness that God has forgiven all people on earth for all their sins. No matter how heinous, no matter how brutal the acts, I was told that each person has been forgiven. During these sessions I also had the phenomenal experience of knowing that I had been forgiven for all the harm I had done to others.

At another time, through another method, I gained the knowledge that I was no better or worse than any other human being on earth. I saw myself lying down next to the man who molested me and felt this awareness in a profound way. He and I were the same, no different. We had both harmed other people; my abusiveness was no less damaging than his. These two experiences together changed me irrevocably. I now understood that we are all the same in the eyes of God—we are all sinners and all sinners are forgiven—*absolutely*.

You may believe that surely some people's sins are worse (i.e., more harmful) than others. It is not my intention here to try to make you change your beliefs but only to pass on an important spiritual insight I feel privileged to have received.

This doesn't mean that we won't pay for our sins; nor should our sins be excused. We should and will be accountable one way or another.

There is a time for forgiveness and a time to withhold forgiveness. If attempting to forgive causes you more harm than not forgiving, it isn't time to forgive. Even though the benefits to forgiveness cannot be denied, for some not forgiving is the healthiest choice they can make. Above all, you must be the one to decide whether you are ready, willing, and able to forgive. Don't allow anyone to pressure you into a false forgiveness or shame you into feeling bad that you can't forgive. If it is right for you, forgiveness will come. When it does, it will change your life. Until then, give yourself permission to be wherever you are.

PART FOUR

Learn How to Ask for an Apology

CHAPTER 8

Silence Isn't Always Golden

Anger is often more harmful than the injury that caused it.
ENGLISH PROVERB

THE POWER OF APOLOGY PRINCIPLE 8

Remaining silent instead of asking for an apology from those who have hurt you can cause as many problems in relationships as not apologizing when you have hurt someone.

As important as giving and receiving apologies is to our emotional and physical well-being, asking for an apology is equally important. *Remaining silent, building up resentments, and distancing yourself from others instead of letting them know how they have hurt you can cause as many problems in interpersonal relationships as not apologizing when you have hurt someone.* Even though you may pride yourself on your willingness and ability to admit when you are wrong and to apologize when you've hurt others, if you aren't also able to let others know when you feel they owe you an apology you will contribute to relationship problems as much as those who are unable or unwilling to apologize. To make matters worse, by not asking for the apologies you feel you are owed, you actually reinforce a non-apologizer's tendency to avoid taking responsibility. With your silence you encourage others to continue treating you in inconsiderate, selfish, or even abusive ways.

Often it is the case that the person who has offended you is oblivious to the fact that he or she did anything to hurt your feelings. As much as it may have felt like a knife piercing your heart, to the other person it may have seemed like nothing. He or she may not even be aware that anything at all transpired between the two of you.

For example, my client, Kelly, recently came into her session angry because her best friend had hurt her feelings. Kelly explained that her friend had been complaining about her children and said, "It's a good thing you don't have any kids. You don't know how lucky you are."

Kelly was devastated. "She knows how hard my husband and I have been trying to have a baby, and the heartache we've been feeling because we aren't able to. How could she say such an insensitive thing to me!" She continued: "I've been avoiding her for almost a week. I don't return her phone calls and I'm seriously thinking about ending our friendship entirely. Who needs such an insensitive person in their life?"

As we talked further, I brought up the possibility of Kelly telling her friend about how the comment hurt her and asking her friend for an apology. At first Kelly bristled, saying she shouldn't be the one asking for the apology, that her friend should be the one offering it. "Why should I lower myself and go to her? She's the one who is wrong. She needs to come to me."

Then I suggested that her friend might not even realize that her comment had hurt Kelly. "How could she not know?" Kelly countered. "And if she doesn't know, that makes her even more insensitive." I didn't argue with Kelly on this point, but I did suggest that whether she decided to continue the relationship or not, it would probably make her feel a lot better if she expressed her hurt to her friend.

We went on to other related issues and nothing more was said about Kelly's friend or the incident for several weeks. Then, three sessions later, Kelly told me that she had, in fact, decided to tell her friend about her hurtful comment:

I started missing her and I realized she probably didn't know she'd hurt me. She sounded so confused on her phone messages, like she didn't have a clue what was wrong. I called her up and said I wanted to talk. She came right over. When I told her how her comment had really hurt me, she looked confused for a few minutes and then said, "Gosh, did I say that? How insensitive! I'm so sorry. Of course that must have hurt you. I know how much you want a baby. You know what an idiot I can be sometimes. I just wasn't thinking."

It was so simple. In just a few minutes the whole thing was over. I knew she was sorry and the issue of her being insensitive wasn't really an issue any longer. To think I was willing to end our friendship over one insensitive remark! I'm so glad I had the nerve to tell her why I was hurt.

By taking the first step and letting the person know how he or she hurt you, you show great courage and a willingness to talk things out. You give the other person important information about what you like and don't like so that he or she won't be likely to offend you again in the same way. And you will probably feel a lot better than you did when you were stewing about what the wrongdoer did and how he or she didn't even have the decency to apologize.

Those who have asked for an apology and had the situation clarified, as in the above example, tend to continue doing so as a common practice. They've learned that it feels a lot better to make the first move and to clear the air rather than to demonize a wrongdoer. That was the situation with Kelly. Having had such success with her friend, Kelly made a major change in the way she handles similar situations. Now, when someone hurts her feelings, she tells the person about it and asks for an apology if it isn't forthcoming. Because of this new way of dealing with people, she is not the angry person she once was and has fewer ongoing conflicts with others.

Even in situations where you know the other person is aware of offending you but has chosen not to apologize, making the first move can be the smart thing to do. It often happens that once you've brought the offense out in the open and explained to the other person how much pain you felt about the situation, the offending party has a chance to reflect and may begin to feel actual remorse. The result may be that he or she is then able to give you a genuine apology.

Even if the person refuses to apologize, your efforts were not in vain. By speaking up, you are sending a strong message that you do not appreciate or approve of his or her behavior. This usually has an effect on people. Even if they are too proud to apologize or admit they were wrong, the average person will think twice before repeating the act in your presence.

Those who continue to behave in ways that make you uncomfortable are sending *you* a strong message. They are saying they don't respect your wishes and don't care about your feelings. When this happens, you now have valuable information about this person and your relationship. Whether you wish to act on it will be up to you, but if you respect yourself you will likely limit your relationship with this person or end it all together.

Be Willing to Forgive Before Asking for an Apology

Just as you should never apologize until you have forgiven, you should never ask for an apology unless you are willing to forgive. Otherwise, it is an exercise in futility at the very least, and at the most it is a power play on your part. The whole point of asking for an apology is for you to find out whether the person who wronged you is truly remorseful so that you can open your heart and move toward forgiveness. It is not to force another person to humble herself before you so that you can feel you have power over her.

While it is true that hearing the apology will make you better able to forgive, you need to do your part by being willing to forgive. Otherwise, no matter how sincerely the offending party apologizes, you may not be able to forgive. Your pride, your anger, and your need for revenge will get in the way and you will sabotage your opportunity for healing. Since you aren't likely to ask for a second apology, nor is the wrongdoer likely to give one, make sure you are ready to forgive before asking.

How to Ask for an Apology

If you feel someone owes you an apology, instead of pining away or letting your anger fester, *ask* for it.

1. Start by stating, "I feel you owe me an apology for . . . ," or "In order to forgive you (or reconcile with you), I need you to apologize."

2. Specifically state the reason you feel you are owed an apology and explain how the other person's actions or inactions affected you.

3. State what else you need in order to forgive (e.g., "I need you to promise you won't do it again"; "I need you to get some professional help so that you will understand why you did what you did").

By asking for an apology you give those you care about the benefit of the doubt. Instead of assuming the worst in someone or robbing this person of the opportunity to make a positive change, let the wrongdoer know he or she hurt or disappointed you.

Never underestimate the power of communicating with someone about an offense. Communication can cause people to think about their behavior in ways they might never have done had you not spoken up. It gives the person the opportunity to not only apologize for his or her behavior but to make sure he or she doesn't make the same mistake or commit the same offense again. The person may begin thinking about others he has offended in the same way. It may even encourage him to acknowledge his wrongs and seek forgiveness from others.

The following suggestions may help you in your endeavor:

1. Be selective. Don't ask for an apology for every little mistake or faux pas. Save your requests for offenses that really hurt you or damage the relationship.

2. Make sure you don't approach the other person with arrogance or self-righteousness. It's always possible that you may have misunderstood someone or misinterpreted his or her actions.

3. Before you ask for an apology, make clear in your own mind what you want out of the experience. For example, ask yourself the following questions:

   - How do I want the person to apologize (in person, by letter)?

   - What words do I need to hear ("I'm sorry," "I apologize," "Please forgive me")?

   - Do I also need the person to make restitution in some way (e.g., financial restitution, a promise to never repeat the act, a particular action such as entering therapy, proof that he or she has changed in some way)?

- How will I know if he or she is sincere?
- How will I know if he or she has learned a lesson?

Connect with Your Pain

Simply telling someone you are angry with him or her tends to put that person on the defensive. But underneath the anger usually lies pain. If you can connect with that pain and tell the wrongdoer why you feel you are owed an apology, you will usually find that he or she is less defensive and more willing to see your point of view and feel empathy toward you. For example, pay attention to the difference in tone of these two statements:

1. "Why didn't you call me last night? It really made me angry."
2. "When you didn't call me last night, I felt hurt. I'd like an explanation and an apology."

The first statement is likely to put the other person on the defensive. We don't want someone to be angry with us, so we are more likely to defend ourselves or try to assuage the anger than to apologize about not calling.

The second statement, while possibly not as assertive, is likely to elicit an entirely different response. Most people are caught off guard when you tell them that their behavior hurt your feelings. They immediately feel like apologizing to help soothe the hurt. Instead of feeling defensive, the other person is far more likely to allow herself to express vulnerability and to explain why she didn't call, not in order to defend herself but to help you see she didn't intend to hurt your feelings.

Of course, admitting that your feelings were hurt, while getting right to the core of the problem, requires you to be vulnerable. This is uncomfortable for many people. It is far easier to be angry. Unless you have issues with being unable to express anger, or a tendency to see yourself as a victim, allowing yourself to feel and express this vulnerability will cause your communication with others to become far more constructive than if you barraged them with your anger.

Asking for an apology is also a way of showing assertiveness. By calling someone's attention to the fact that he or she hurt or offended you, you also send the message that you will not allow anyone to treat you poorly, as the following story illustrates.

The Boy with a Lot of Courage and a Lot of Self-Esteem

A woman in one of my groups told me the story of how her son came to demand an apology from a teacher. It seems that the teacher had singled her son out in front of the class by telling him that he just wasn't "getting" what she was trying to teach. Her son felt humiliated. But instead of just letting it go and allowing her words to affect his self-esteem, he decided to do something about it.

A few days later, armed with a stack of his graded papers, he confronted the teacher after class. "Miss Brown," he said, "I want you to know that I *am* getting what you're teaching and I have the papers here to prove it." The teacher looked at the papers and told my client's son that she agreed with him. "You're right, Tommy. These papers show that you are understanding the class. I shouldn't have said that to you." But that wasn't enough for this brave boy. He then demanded a public apology in front of the class. Impressed with his courage and determination, the teacher did just that.

The teacher later told his mother, "He's a brave boy who knows how to take care of himself."

By speaking up instead of ignoring the fact that his teacher had been insensitive, Tommy found a way of mending his hurt feelings and standing up for his rights.

Asking for an Apology When You Have No Contact

There are many people who long for an apology but have little hope of ever receiving one because of lost contact or death. Unfortunately, not everyone has the experience of receiving an apology from those who have hurt them. But this doesn't mean they can't experience the healing benefits of apology. By using the following strategy, even those who never receive an actual apology can experience its healing power.

EXERCISE
Your Fantasy Apology

A. Write a letter to the person who wronged you outlining the offense and asking him or her for an apology.

B. Now write a letter from the perspective of the person who wronged you, saying the words you've longed to hear. Write in the way you would have liked the person to have responded, including such aspects as how much he regretted what he did and how much he wished he had been able to apologize to you before he died.

Many people have reported that the apology they received in this exercise felt almost as good as a real apology. This may or may not be your experience, but you'll benefit from asking for the apology or from the empathy you gain by imagining the other person's response.

Learning to ask for an apology can be just as important and just as difficult as learning how to apologize. It takes courage to stand up to those who have hurt you and to let them know how you feel. It takes caring and commitment to a relationship to bring things out in the open instead of ending the relationship or distancing from the person who has wronged you. Whether your purpose in asking someone for an apology is to take a stand in order to let someone know that you are unwilling to be treated a certain way, or to prevent yourself from holding onto your anger and letting it poison a relationship, your cause is a worthy one and well worth the effort. Encourage yourself to keep asking for apologies even if your first efforts don't turn out the way you wished and give yourself credit when you've had the courage to continue trying.

PART FIVE

Transform All Your Relationships Through Apology

CHAPTER 9

Healing Your Relationship with Yourself

He who knows others is wise;
He who knows himself is enlightened.

LAO-TZU

And why beholdest thou the mote that is in thy brother's eye,
but considerest not the beam that is in thine own eye?

MATTHEW 7:2–3

Apology has the power to transform us all into more honest, compassionate, and full human beings. In this chapter we explore how, by taking responsibility for our actions, apologizing to those we have harmed, honoring the reactions of others, and being open when someone asks for an apology from us, we can heal our relationship with ourselves, which is truly the most important relationship we have.

Apology teaches us important lessons. It teaches us to take responsibility for our actions, it teaches us humility, and it reminds us that our words and actions have consequences. Apology teaches us that we do not have to be perfect and encourages us to have tolerance toward others and ourselves. Finally, it teaches us compassion and empathy toward others. These can be the most significant lessons we can learn in a lifetime.

The Lesson of Taking Responsibility

Taking responsibility for your actions instead of denying responsibility or blaming others can transform all your relationships, most importantly, your relationship with yourself. When you do the honorable thing—accept responsibility for your actions and apologize to those you've harmed—you increase your respect for yourself, which in turn increases your self-esteem and self-confidence.

Some people always manage to turn things around and make it the other person's fault: "She made me act like that," or, "If only he hadn't pushed me into it." But while denial and blame may at times keep us from having to experience the consequences of our actions, they create some very negative consequences of their own.

First, denying and blaming keep us from growing, from learning from our mistakes. The most profound emotional changes come from facing the consequences of our offenses against others.

Second, continually denying responsibility and blaming others causes other people to lose respect for us. People aren't stupid—they eventually see past our lies and excuses, seeing us for who we really are.

Shame and Self-Esteem

One of the most significant gifts that taking responsibility can offer us is to help us heal our problems with shame. If you carry around too much shame, taking responsibility for your actions and apologizing to those you've harmed is the best remedy. Dwelling on mistakes doesn't help anyone, including the person you harmed.

Apology can remove the cloak of shame that even the most remorseful person carries around. When we apologize, it is as if a burden has been lifted off our shoulders and we can once again appreciate the positive things about ourselves. We feel redeemed in our own eyes.

If we don't experience sufficient shame when we wrong someone else, apology can help remind us of the harm we caused. The act of having to apologize to someone usually causes us to feel humiliated.

Remembering that humiliation the next time we are tempted to repeat the same act can discourage us from acting on impulse.

Taking responsibility for our actions instills pride and self-respect. We feel better about ourselves when we do the right thing. Even though we may feel more shame at the moment, when we admit we were wrong and apologize for our behavior that feeling of shame will be replaced before long with a feeling of self-respect and genuine pride (as opposed to false pride).

The Lesson of Honoring the Reactions of Others

Many of us go through life focusing our attention outward, finding fault in others, blaming others whenever there is a conflict. But this is the easy way out. It is far too easy to pass the buck each time we are involved in a disagreement or conflict with someone. It's far too easy to assess blame elsewhere than to look inside ourselves to discover our own faults. By focusing outward, we rob ourselves not only of healthy, truly intimate relationships but also of the insights and growth that can come from self-reflection and self-assessment.

When someone else's feelings have been hurt by our actions, whether our behavior was intentional or not, conscious or not, we have an obligation to address the issue and their reaction. This concept is controversial, since for decades we have been taught that we are *not responsible* for the reactions of others. For example, in the 1960s during the human potential movement we were taught that we don't ever *cause* another person to feel anything. In the 1970s and 1980s, New Age and metaphysical teachings espoused the idea that we *choose* to react in a certain way and that therefore no one can cause us to feel anything. Beliefs such as *we choose our own reality* have now morphed into the current attitude among many, especially the young, that we can do anything we want and the reactions of others be damned. Today when adolescents are asked "How do you feel about the fact that your behavior worries your parents?," the common answer is "I don't care" or "I didn't ask them to worry."

While there is some truth to the belief that we are not responsible for the reactions and feelings of others, we are responsible for our behavior and the consequences of our behavior. If, in fact, it was our behavior that caused another person to feel hurt, afraid, or angry, we have an obligation to deal with his or her reaction.

If I hurt someone's feelings, whether I intended to or not, the respectful, caring thing for me to do is to listen while the person explains to me why my behavior hurt him or her. Then I can either choose to take responsibility for my actions and apologize, or at the very least explain that my behavior was not intentional and that I am sorry for any hurt I caused.

According to McCullough, Sandage, and Worthington, the authors of *To Forgive Is Human*, today few of us belong to communities that have clear, consistent norms for right and wrong behavior. When we experience guilt, most of us don't look for visible community standards that we might have violated. We don't undergo a judgment by a community (unless we break a law). We don't have a community to prescribe a course of action that we should take to right our wrong. And afterward no community receives us back as members in good standing.

This primarily leaves it up to the individual to determine when and if he or she has harmed another person (with the exception of when he or she has broken the law). Today, unless someone confronts us with our behavior, many of us never realize we have harmed another person.

Begin to View Confrontations as Opportunities

When your behavior has caused someone to feel hurt, afraid, or angry, and he or she is able to tell you about it, it is an opportunity for you to learn about yourself. If you are in an important relationship with this person, whether it is a personal or business relationship, it is also an excellent opportunity for you to deepen the trust in your relationship.

When someone has the courage to confront you about your behavior, see this as the gift that it is. The alternative would be for the other person to remain silent about his or her feelings and to distance from you. And unless someone tells us about our behavior, what chance do we have to change it? Instead we continue to behave in the same way, alienating others and never understanding why.

Look for Patterns

Once someone has confronted you with your behavior, begin looking for patterns in your relationships, particularly patterns concerning your everyday conflicts with others. For example, let's say that every time you have a relationship with someone younger than yourself (personal or business), the relationship becomes fraught with conflict and tension and the younger person ends up confronting you about your behavior. You could continue to assume that the conflicts are always the younger person's fault. After all, young people can be selfish, short-sighted, and unappreciative of the wisdom of their elders. However, do you really think it is a coincidence that you tend to have conflicts with younger people? Isn't it just as possible that you are the one with the problem? That there is something about younger people that bothers you, something inside you that becomes unsettled?

Perhaps it is their very youth that bothers you. Since you are getting older yourself, perhaps you resent young people because they have their entire future ahead of them, whereas you are becoming painfully aware of how little time you have left to accomplish the goals you set for yourself. Perhaps you resent the self-centeredness of youth because when you were growing up you didn't have a chance to be selfish. Maybe you were responsible for others (your younger siblings, your own children, etc.) at a very early age or you had a job at an early age. And perhaps the sense of entitlement that so many young people have irritates you because you were raised to believe that you had to do everything on your own, that you shouldn't ask anyone for help or expect help from anyone.

We all have unresolved issues—with our parents, with the opposite sex, with those who remind us of people who ignored, bullied, or betrayed us in the past. And we are all constantly placing the pictures of our past enemies onto the faces of those in our present (another form of projection). Unfortunately, when we do this we are unable to see the real person with whom we are dealing, nor are we able to take responsibility for our own actions. Our past conflicts blind us to what is actually occurring in the present relationship.

There Are Two Sides to Every Story

If we take the courageous step of acknowledging to ourselves that there really are two sides to every story and that each person's perceptions of the situation are made up of both truth and distortions, we will be more willing to entertain the idea that we do, indeed, owe someone an apology, even when our first response is to immediately reject the idea.

There is nothing more insulting than being told we owe someone an apology when we are the ones who feel wronged. *How dare
she think I should apologize. She should be down on her knees begging me
for my forgiveness.* But if someone confronts us with our behavior, no
matter how far off the mark this person may seem to be, there is a
lesson to be learned. The lesson may not be apparent, but with
some time and some soul searching we are likely to dig it up.

Our life lessons come in interesting forms and often the mes-
sengers are those who give us the most trouble—the pest who won't
go away but continually insists we wronged him or her, the person
who constantly misunderstands us, the person who constantly irritates us, the person who angers or repulses us the most. The next
time you have an experience with such a person, ask yourself the following questions:

1. Is there a pattern here? Have I had the same kind of conflict
   with others in the past? About the same issues? Or, do I continually have conflicts with the same type of person (same sex,
   same age, same type of personality).

2. When was the last time I had a similar conflict with someone?
   What are the commonalities?

3. Have other people complained to me about the same behavior on my part?

4. How do I normally go about resolving my conflicts? Who, if
   anyone, ends up apologizing?

5. Do I always feel like the injured party when I am in conflict
   with someone, or do I tend to feel like the villain?

Spend some time carefully thinking about these questions before
you answer them. Writing down your answers may also reveal some
deeper insights into your past and your psyche.

The Lesson of Humility

In addition to apology encouraging us to take responsibility for our
actions and our patterns, it teaches us humility, which many of us
need to learn. Some of us are so arrogant that we truly believe we
are always right. We have built up such a false sense of pride that we
feel everything we do is great and no one can match our intellect,
talents, beauty, and so forth.

Apology humbles even the most arrogant of people. This is partly why it is so important for some people to receive an apology, particularly in cases where a criminal or other offender has adamantly denied responsibility for his or her actions. When an offender is arrogant in addition to causing harm to someone, it feels like a slap in the face to the victims. Not only were they harmed by the offender's actions but by his or her present attitude. Time after time, we hear of cases where the victim states that if the offender would apologize, he or she would be willing to drop the charges. Remember how, after the guilty verdict in the civil trial of O. J. Simpson, the father of Ronald Goldman stated that if O. J. would admit guilt he would forfeit the award issued by the court? At that point, after enduring O. J.'s arrogance for months on end, it probably would have been worth millions of dollars to see him humbled.

The same is true of the Clinton case. How many times did you hear people say, "If he would just genuinely say he's sorry . . . ?" In order to forgive him, we wanted him to humble himself before us.

The price you will personally pay for holding onto your arrogance and refusing to admit when you are wrong can be the loss of your marriage, the respect of your children, and the respect of those with whom you work. And the biggest price of all is the loss of your true self. The more you build up walls of arrogance in order to protect your pride, the less contact you have with your true self. Ultimately, the false self you show the world—the person who is always confident, always right, always on top of things—will take over and you will have little or no true self to come home to.

Apology has the power to bring down the wall of even the most arrogant, defensive person. When we apologize, we humble ourselves before the person we have harmed, and this helps us to regain our dignity and our humanity.

The Lesson of Accepting Our Imperfections

Since we are all flawed human beings, we can never expect ourselves to be perfect. In fact, it is when we expect ourselves to be perfect or when others expect it of us that we get into trouble. Carl Jung, the psychoanalyst, proposed the concept of the Shadow or our dark side—a part of us that is created when we attempt to be perfect, when we try to deny our darker urges such as greed, lust, and dishonesty.

As human beings, we contain within ourselves a whole spectrum of urges and potential behaviors, but our parents, society, and religion reinforce some and discourage others. Although it is important for children to learn certain social behaviors in the process of growing up, the very act of encouraging some while discouraging others creates within us a Shadow personality. These rejected qualities do not cease to exist simply because they've been denied direct expression. Instead, they live on within us and form the secondary personality that psychology calls the *Shadow*.

Making apologies allows us to be imperfect. While it doesn't take away the hurt we can cause by our impatience, lack of consideration, pettiness, selfishness, or unreasonable expectations of others, it does provide us with an opportunity to make amends to those we have hurt, to express our remorse, our caring, and our intention to do better. This is far better than trying to do the impossible—to be perfect. In fact, by attempting to be perfect we actually create within ourselves a much larger dark side or Shadow.

By acknowledging, admitting, and ultimately accepting our socalled negative qualities, we take them out of the Shadow and into the light, where they are far less powerful and far less likely to eat away at us and cause us to feel self-critical. By the same token, if we get past our black-and-white thinking, we will understand that making a mistake does not make us a bad person.

The Lesson of Self-Forgiveness

Criticizing and judging ourselves keeps us down, robs us of our confidence and motivation to change, and prevents us from learning from our mistakes. It encourages others to judge us and keeps us in negative situations and around negative people far longer than we should stay.

Whether the person you apologize to is willing to forgive you or finds that he or she is unable to do so, you will still need to forgive yourself. Even if you have been able to apologize or make amends to those you have wronged and have been forgiven by them, you will still need to work toward forgiving yourself. And even those who feel forgiven by God or their higher power often need to forgive themselves.

At the moment of near death many people experience an instantaneous life review. Many would say this occurs so that God or some cosmic judge and jury can determine their place in heaven or hell, or decide whether they are to return to earth again, and if so, in what form. But others believe it is to allow them to appreciate what they have learned and to discover what they have yet to learn. Most especially, they can see whether their actions spread love and whether they learned compassion. Rather than a collection of deeds, people report that the life review is centered on emotions. The consequences of their actions as they affected other people are revealed through the perspective of the people with whom they interacted. While this is occurring, people report being surrounded by the light of forgiveness and knowing that they are forgiven by God. The question is whether they can forgive themselves.

A Seven-Step Process of Self-Forgiveness

1. Admit to yourself that you were wrong or you made a mistake.
2. Write about the consequences of your behavior. Who did you hurt and in what ways?
3. Take responsibility for your actions, regardless of what led you to them.
4. Confess your mistake or wrongdoing to your Creator, yourself, and another person or group of people (a 12-step group, a therapist, or a spiritual leader).
5. Ask God (or your higher power) for help.
6. Make amends for your actions by apologizing to the person you hurt and making restitution to the person you hurt in the best way possible (offer to pay for his or her therapy, pay back the debt, etc.).
7. Look for the lesson. Learn from your mistake so that you do not repeat it. Seek psychological or spiritual help if needed so that you do not repeat the same mistake.

If you have learned from your mistake and do not wish to repeat it, then you no longer need to feel guilty about it. Forgive yourself and let it go.

If you find you are still overwhelmed with guilt about how your past behavior has affected someone, it is important to realize and remember this truth: *The most effective method of self-forgiveness is for you to vow that you will not continue the same behavior and not hurt someone in the same way again.*

Finally, it is important to realize that we are all teachers. Without error on someone's part, none of us would learn the lesson of compassion that forgiveness brings. There is a Buddhist idea that suffering exists specifically to teach us compassion. This idea can help us to face our actions so that we can go on to forgive ourselves for the hurts we have caused other people and forgive them for the hurts they have caused us.

CHAPTER 10

Healing Your Past, Step 1: Make Your Apology List

A lot of people mistake a short memory for a clear conscience.

DOUG LARSON

A long habit of thinking a thing wrong gives it a superficial appearance of being right.

THOMAS PAINE

A half-truth is a whole lie.

YIDDISH PROVERB

Apologizing and asking for apologies are, by far, the most effective ways of healing our past. The information in this chapter will help you if you wish to apologize to those you've hurt, disappointed, or harmed in the past, as well as if you wish to ask for an apology from those who have wronged you.

I'll also help those of you who are in the process of reviewing your life—either because you are in midlife, in a 12-step program, or reaching the end of your life—to make a list of those you've harmed and to decide to whom you need to make amends.

Review Your Life

As we begin to reach midlife and beyond, many of us tend to look back more than we look forward. In fact, as Gail Sheehy outlines in her book, *Passages*, midlife is when we turn our focus inward. Since most people have established their careers and families by this time, they have more time and energy available to address unresolved life issues. Midlife becomes the time to:

- Review your life.
- Resolve issues with your family of origin.
- Make amends or apologize for past deeds and oversights.

The same is true for those who have been diagnosed with a life-threatening disease, those coming to the end of their life, and those who have survived a major crisis, trauma, or illness. It is at these times that most people become more appreciative of life and of the people in their life. Many come to realize that their relationships with family and friends are far more important than success or the accumulation of material things. And many people reassess their lives and realize that petty disagreements aren't very important after all.

As I discussed in my book, *Blessings of the Fall*, one of the greatest advantages of a fall from grace is that it can often cause the fallen to review and reevaluate their life. The experience of a fall, a crisis, or a near-death experience often causes people to see their lives "flash before their eyes," much like a near-death experience.

Dannion Brinkley, in *Saved by the Light*, recalled during his near-death experience: "The Being of Light engulfed me, and as it did I began to experience my whole life, feeling and seeing everything that had ever happened to me. It was as though a dam had burst and every memory stored in my brain flowed out."

Starting with what Brinkley called his "angry childhood," he was forced to witness each and every negative, cruel, or selfish act he had ever committed against another person. He saw himself mercilessly teasing other children, hitting teachers, and stealing bicycles.

Each time he relived an incident he found himself experiencing the pain of those he had hurt. This time, when he remembered a fistfight, he felt the anguish and humiliation his opponent had felt. He also felt the grief he had caused his parents with his delinquent behavior.

"As my body lay dead on that stretcher, I was reliving every moment of my life, including my emotions, attitudes, and motivations." Not only could he actually experience the way both he and the other person had felt when an incident took place, but he could also feel the emotions of the next person indirectly affected by his behavior: "I was in a chain reaction of emotion, one that showed how deeply we affect one another."

Like Brinkley, many others who have had this type of near-death experience report it to be a life-transforming one. But you don't need to wait until a crisis or a fall to review your life and discover to whom you need to make amends. I too came to review my life, take a close look at how I had treated others, and face some important things about myself. Although less dramatic than Dannion Brinkley's near-death experience, mine was equally sobering. I too came to vividly remember all the damage I had done to others and to experience their pain, disappointment, and anger.

I remembered all the people who had been kind to me, but whom, in my arrogant, narcissistic fashion, I had taken for granted, been insensitive, and in some instances, even been cruel. I recalled, from a totally different perspective, my past love relationships, and realized that while I had always seen myself as a victim, in most cases I was not. In fact, in some cases I was even the abuser. There had been people who had truly loved me and I had returned their love with jealousy, possessiveness, and endless demands.

Like Dannion Brinkley, I learned that love is the most important thing in life, and I had been too busy demanding it from others to be able to give it. While I gave understanding and compassion to my clients, I did not give the same to my loved ones, most especially to my own mother.

The following exercise will help you to begin your own life review, to take stock of your life and own up to the hurt and pain you may have caused others.

EXERCISE
See Your Life in Review

A. Set up a space for yourself where you will not be disturbed. I recommend lying down in a darkened room, but you may choose to sit up. Put paper and a pen where you can easily reach them. Please read the following instructions through completely before beginning. Once you have them clear in your mind, you can begin the exercise.

1. Take some deep breaths and clear your mind of all thoughts. Think of your life as if it were a movie. Imagine that you have a magic button you can push that will "rewind" your life, much like the rewind button on your remote control. Keep going back until you have reached the memory of the very first time you hurt someone in a significant way. Allow yourself to stay with this memory for a while. Pay attention to the feelings you experience as you recall the incident. Don't move from your position, but pick up your pad of paper and briefly write down a simple notation to remind you of the incident or person.

2. Put your pad down and once again close your eyes. Go forward now in your mind and remember another significant time when you hurt someone. Once again, stay with the memory and with the feelings, and write down a notation on your pad to help you remember it.

3. Continue playing your movie (your life) in your mind, picking out the most significant times in your life when you hurt someone.

4. Open your eyes, pick up your pad, and go over your list of notations, making notes and clarifying them so that you won't forget your memories later.

5. Take some time now while the memories are still clear in your mind and write about each incident, noting the emotions you felt as you came to realize how much you hurt someone.

6. Now put yourself in the other person's place, imagining how he or she felt. To the best of your ability, experience the pain, humiliation, and anger that the other person must have felt.

7. Put a star beside each of the memories that stand out the most—the ones that move you to apologize to the person, the ones where you feel the most shame, guilt, or pain with the realization of how you hurt this person.

Depending on what your apology strategy is, these may be the first people to whom you apologize.

B. On a piece of paper or in your journal, write about the experience from the other person's perspective. Write about how your actions or inaction affected the person emotionally—how you disappointed him, hurt him, or angered him. Writing from the other person's point of view, elaborate on other consequences that your actions or inaction had on this person's life. For example, this is what I imagine one of the people I hurt might have written: *Because of what Beverly did to me, I found I had a difficult time trusting others. I didn't have another relationship for several years, and when I did, I had a difficult time opening up and trusting my partner.*

You may discover that empathy does not come easily to you. If this is the case, you may have to teach yourself to have empathy for others. You can do this by practicing putting yourself in the other person's place, imagining what he or she must have felt, and trying to experience what this person must have experienced.

C. In addition to suddenly becoming aware of the effect they have had on others and remembering cruel or heartless things they've done, the life review enables some people to face other things about themselves they have never faced before. Take more time and write the answers to the following questions in your journal:

1. What have you learned from this experience?

2. How has this experience changed you?

Your life review will obviously take some time. You may be able to get through only one segment of your life (your childhood, your twenties, your thirties, etc.) at a time. You may also become so emotional over one particular memory that you need to stop the exercise and allow yourself to process the memory completely. If either one of these circumstances occurs, go ahead and stop the exercise, but make a commitment to do it again at a later time. Don't allow too much time to transpire before returning to your life review, however, since you need the momentum and the emotional intensity that occurs once you are really into the experience to get the most out of it.

Make Your Apology List

If you do not want to take the time to make an exhaustive life review or do not do well with guided imagery exercises, there is another option: making an apology list. Start by listing all the people you have hurt, betrayed, let down, neglected, offended, or wronged in any way (refer back to the lists you've already started), along with a brief explanation of how you wronged them. This will take some time and will require a great deal of thought.

You may notice that you have a great deal of resistance to making your list and you may find all kinds of excuses to put it aside. But if you really want to clear up your past, this is the most important list you will ever make. Notice your resistance, exploring and feeling the emotions underneath it, but continue to gently push yourself to continue working on it.

You will also likely notice that you are in conflict about listing some people. You may waffle back and forth about whether you should include someone's name, since you may feel that your actions toward him or her were warranted, given the fact that he or she hurt you as well. But you need to include the name of every single person you can remember wronging, even those who hurt you first.

It doesn't matter how badly someone has treated you; it is now important that you be completely honest about your part in the problems you experienced. If you did someone any harm at all, you need to list that person and the harm you did.

You may also experience resistance because making such a list is tedious. *After all, you may rationalize, I can't possibly put down the name of every single person I've hurt in my life. That would be impossible and it would take forever.*

Of course, you can't list every single person you've hurt in your entire lifetime. In the first place, you can't remember your entire lifetime and all the people with whom you've had contact. Primarily I'm talking about listing all those people with whom you've had a *relationship*, those who touched your life in a significant way. This will include family, friends, co-workers, employers and employees, and business associates, as well as people who looked up to you (students, trainees, supervisees, those you coached or mentored).

Of course, in some instances, you will also need to include people with whom you had no relationship whatsoever but to whom your actions or inactions caused suffering. For example, if you had an affair with a married man who has children, you will need to include his wife and children on your list. If you were driving drunk and hit a car full of people, you will need to include every person in the car as well as their family members. If you embezzled money from your job, you will need to include all of the owners of the company and their families.

We will call this list your *primary* apology list. Your primary list will be the list on which you will focus most of your attention. From this list you will create an *apology plan*.

What to Do If You Are Stuck

Some people have difficulty coming up with a list of those they have wronged. They may be able to think of only a few people; in rare instances, some won't be able to think of anyone. If this is your situation, rest assured that there have, in fact, been those you've wronged—you just aren't able to think of them for one reason or another.

Some have trouble figuring out what actions are actually harmful to another person. As noted in 12-step literature, ironically, the question of how to identify harm rarely arises when we're remembering the harm done to us by others. We have no trouble whatsoever remembering and spelling out what actions by others have caused us harm! If you are struggling with the question *What is harm?* the following exercise will help you.

EXERCISE
Identify Harm

A. Write a list of some of the ways in which you've been hurt by others.

B. Now, go over your list item by item and ask yourself, *Have I ever dealt with another person in a similar way?*

❧

By honestly answering this question for each item on their list, most people are surprised to discover that they have hurt others in the same ways that they themselves have been hurt.

The following exercises will help to further jog your memory and to clarify exactly who you should have on your list.

E X E R C I S E
Jogging Your Memory

A. Make a list of all the people you were once close to but are no longer.

B. List the reasons why you are no longer close to each person listed. What happened?

C. Now list the names of the people you are estranged from due to a disagreement, conflict, or whatever.

D. Write down the reasons for the estrangement.

❧

You may or may not feel that you have hurt or wronged those you are estranged from, especially if you were the one who stopped seeing or talking to the person because of something he or she did to you. And just because you are no longer close to someone doesn't necessarily mean you have hurt that person in some way. People can fade out of our lives for many different reasons—we've changed emotionally, we've moved or they did, or we've changed jobs or lost interest in a once mutual pastime or sport. But often the real reason for the lack of contact is that you offended them or they offended you.

If they offended you, you probably remember the reason for the split, but if you offended them, you may not. Spend more time thinking about the relationship, what kind of a person you were at the time, and what was going on in your life and theirs.

EXERCISE
Examine Your Negative Qualities

Unfortunately, we are often oblivious to how our behavior and attitudes affect others. This exercise will help you to focus on the personal qualities that you possess that are most likely offensive to others.

A. What is your most negative quality? How do you believe this characteristic has affected those around you, particularly your partner, your children, and your family of origin?

B. Make a list of your most negative qualities and ask yourself the above question for each one.

C. What do you feel most ashamed of in your life? Write about the incident in detail, outlining exactly why you feel ashamed.

D. Who in your life have you hurt the most? Again, write about this in detail, describing exactly how your behavior hurt or damaged the other person.

E. Whose life have you most negatively affected? In detail, write about the effect your behavior had on this person's life.

These lists will no doubt help those who were stuck remembering past offenses and oversights. They will also help those with a substantial primary list to add to it.

These lists will also be used later when you make your list of those to whom you wish to *ask for* an apology. We often write people off who offend or disappoint us instead of asking for an apology.

Finally, for those who are still stuck, here are some possible reasons why you may owe someone an apology:

- Lying
- Being unfaithful
- Taking something that did not belong to you
- Not repaying a loan
- Envying what others have

- Turning your back on someone who was in need
- Being overly critical of someone
- Expecting too much from someone or never being pleased
- Judging or being critical of someone because of their race, religion, ethnicity, sexual orientation, political views, or socioeconomic status

In order to experience how apology has the power to remove your guilt and help heal your life, you must first acknowledge the harm you caused others. Naming your wrongs in this way is the first step toward ridding yourself of the guilt and shame you've been carrying around for years. Facing your wrongs head-on is the first step toward healing your past.

Be honest with yourself as you make your apology list. Don't minimize your wrongs, don't make excuses for yourself, and above all, don't blame someone else for your transgressions. By the same token, don't exaggerate your wrongdoings and make them bigger than they actually are. The point here is not to become overwhelmed with guilt and remorse but to honestly assess your past.

Many have found that their own name needs to be somewhere on their list of those they have harmed. While it is important to admit that you have harmed other people, it is also important to acknowledge that you've harmed yourself. Those in 12-step programs find that becoming willing to make amends to themselves and to forgive themselves for past mistakes has been essential to their recovery from compulsive behavior.

Your Apology Plan

Now you are ready to set up your *apology plan*, which will include the following:

- A chronological listing of all those to whom you wish to apologize. Create this list by ranking those on your apology list, from most harmed to least harmed.
- The way you intend to apologize (in person, in a letter, by phone).
- A timetable spelling out approximately how much time you will need to complete apologizing to those on your primary list.

- How and where you plan on seeking support before, during, and after your apologies.

❡

It's very difficult to honestly face the truth concerning how your actions, inactions, and attitudes have harmed others. And it is even more difficult to think about confessing to those you've harmed. But it is important to realize that you are not alone. Everyone has wronged or harmed other people, and everyone needs to apologize and make restitution to those they've harmed.

Unfortunately, not everyone has the courage to face the truth about how they've harmed others and to apologize to those they've harmed. If you are able to do this, you will be one of the few courageous souls to make a significant step toward righting your wrongs, healing your past, and healing the past of those you've hurt. For that you can be proud.

CHAPTER 11

Healing Your Past, Step 2: Make Amends

True confession consists in telling our deed in such a way that our soul is changed in the telling of it.

MAUDE PETRE

Don't look where you fell, but where you slipped.

LIBERIAN PROVERB

Forgive everything.

MORRIE *(TUESDAYS WITH MORRIE)*

Making amends is doing more than simply apologizing. It means doing something to change the situation, to do everything within our power to right our wrongs or to repair the harm we have caused. If we have lied to someone, we set the record straight by telling the truth (as long as we can do so without causing further harm). If we have stolen from someone, damaged property, cost someone money due to our actions, or in some other way materially or financially harmed others, we either pay them back or make arrangements to pay the money we owe. If we have physically or emotionally harmed others in such a way that they needed to seek medical or psychiatric help, we offer to pay for their medical or counseling bills.

As most people who have completed a 12-step recovery program have discovered, making amends is one of the most liberating experiences of their life. Making amends should include:

- Apologizing
- Acknowledging the specific harm you've done
- Making appropriate restitution
- Changing your behavior toward the other person in the future

How to Make the Most of Your Attempt at Making Amends

Even though you realize you have caused other people harm and are sorry for what you've done, confessing your wrongdoings to the people you've harmed may seem like a humiliating and frightening thing to do. For this reason, it is important to rehearse your amends ahead of time. Planning what you are going to say and how you are going to say it will make the idea of actually making your amends a little less frightening. You may want to rehearse with a friend, a therapist, or if you are in a 12-step program, with your sponsor.

A common obstacle that many people encounter when they attempt to make amends to someone in their past is that their own resentment toward the other person for his or her part in the disagreement or conflict gets in the way. Then they're likely to bring up the other person's mistakes and end up insulting him or her. Thus, it is vitally important that you make sure you have forgiven the other person before attempting to make your amends.

Make Sure Your Amends Benefit All Concerned

You will not necessarily make formal in-person amends to each person on your list. In some cases, you can do more harm than good by facing people directly and talking to them about hurtful situations from the past. For example, if someone is very old or very ill, bringing up the past, especially if it is quite painful, may end up being far too upsetting and even life-threatening. On the other hand, many people are far more receptive to forgiving when they are ill or dying and welcome the chance to complete any unfinished business. It might be a good idea to talk to those who are close to the person to whom you wish to make amends and ask them whether they feel he or she can handle the situation.

Another consideration might be this: Is the other person aware that there is a problem between you? Have you been estranged or have your actions caused distance or tension between you? Or is he or she oblivious to the problem, thinking that your relationship is fine? The purpose of making amends is to help clear away guilt and ill will so that you may establish better relationships with those whom your life has touched. If the other person is oblivious to the fact that you have harmed her or him (as in the case of infidelity), you may wish to choose the timing of your amends very carefully. Deciding to confess your infidelity when your partner or past partner is ill, in the midst of a crisis at work, or about to have a baby can be a selfish and heartless thing to do.

In contrast, if you have been estranged from a close friend or family member due to an action on your part and your inability to apologize, your amends will probably be welcomed almost anytime—that is, unless the other person is in the middle of some kind of crisis or life-changing event. Even then, depending on the circumstances, a long-overdue apology may be just what the person needs to feel better or to make the celebration that much more special.

Never apologize or make amends directly to a person if it means you will likely cause the person more harm by doing so. Here are some examples of when direct amends could be harmful:

- Going to the spouse of someone with whom you had an affair and confessing, especially if the spouse doesn't know about the affair.

- Confessing your *feelings* for someone, for example, going to someone and saying, "Please forgive me. I've been a hypocrite. I've pretended to like you all these years but I really don't." This is inappropriate and will only inflict pain. The appropriate way to make amends in this situation is either to stop being a hypocrite and begin to be more honest in your dealings with the person, or to take a closer look at exactly why you dislike this person (e.g., Is this person showing you an aspect of yourself that you dislike?) and try to work past your dislike. If you have been envious of someone for many years, the appropriate way to make amends is to take a closer look at your envy to find your own rejected or denied potential.

Amends should be made in a way that will benefit all concerned, beginning with the initial contact. The following suggestions will help you:

1. Let go of any expectations you may have regarding how the other person will receive you and how he or she will react to your amends. This is especially important if you tend to fantasize about outcomes. Don't set yourself up for a huge disappointment by fantasizing about some romanticized outcome in which the person you offended welcomes you with open arms and congratulates you on your courage.

   Neither should you expect the worst. Although in most cases you'll probably be treated better than you've anticipated, there is no way to predict a person's reaction. Be prepared for any or all of the following reactions:

   - The other person may be stunned that you are apologizing and not know how to react or what to say.

   - Sometimes people don't even remember that you ever harmed them.

   - The other person may react to your attempt at amends by expressing anger toward you.

   - The other person may not remember or recognize the reasons for your amends but may bring up other things you did to hurt or harm him or her.

   - In rare instances, people sometimes refuse your attempts to apologize.

   If someone does refuse to accept your apology, work on releasing this person and releasing any negative feelings you have toward him or her. We cannot control how others receive our amends—they have the right to hold a grudge against us the rest of their lives if they choose to. Your job is to just make sure you don't hold a grudge against them.

   No one owes us forgiveness. Making your amends will help you to forgive yourself—and that is the most important thing. Having cleared up your side of the relationship, having done what you can to right your wrongs, you no longer need to feel any guilt or anger about the situation. You are free.

2. Your focus should be on clearing up your part in the relationship, not on the other person's reaction. This will require you to be as honest, sincere, and straightforward as you possibly can. Don't beat around the bush and don't try to spare yourself embarrassment by minimizing the harm you've caused. It's not enough to make some vague statement about being sorry for any harm you may have done. You need to state unequivocally that you are aware of the harm that you caused and apologize for that harm. Unless you are specific and direct, you will not communicate sincerity. Even more important, you owe the person you offended an honest and direct acknowledgment of your wrongs.

3. Keep the wording of your apology as simple as possible. Don't bring up details that will only hurt the other person all over again. For example, if you are apologizing for an affair, it is not necessary to bring up the fact that you hadn't felt sexually satisfied with your partner for a long time or that the woman or man with whom you had the affair was so attractive you just couldn't help yourself.

4. Don't make excuses for your behavior. This is dishonest and will only antagonize the other person. No one made you do what you did, no matter how the other person behaved. Take total responsibility for your actions and for harming the other person. If you have done your work on forgiving the other person before you make your amends, you won't need to bring up the other person's mistakes or their part in the problems.

   Later on, in a subsequent discussion, and only if asked, you may wish to share what the circumstances were that led up to the offense. Even then, you must be careful not to blame the victim in any way.

5. It is important that you express your regrets for having harmed the other person in a sincere and serious manner. If you do so grudgingly—just because you think it is the right thing to do—the person you offended will feel your lack of sincerity. If you apologize offhandedly without proper seriousness, the other person will not take your apology all that seriously. It's your job to let the other person know just how much you regret what you did, just how very sorry you are, and how much harm you realize you caused.

For example, if you have been unfaithful and wish to apologize, you might say, "I am sorry for having betrayed you. It was a horrible thing to do to you and to our marriage. I realize it hurt you deeply and it created a huge wedge between us."

If you are apologizing for inappropriate or abusive behavior toward someone, you might say, "I realize I have been far too critical of you and I want to apologize. I know I've hurt you by my critical comments and it was wrong of me to treat you that way."

6. Remember that to amend something means to change it. In most cases, you will need to tell the person to whom you are making the amends what types of changes or restitution you are undertaking. If you are newly aware of how your attitude and behavior have affected others, explain how you came to this realization and what steps you plan on taking to ensure you will not treat people in the same way in the future. If you have begun therapy or a 12-step program, say so. If your behavior has caused another person to enter therapy, offer to pay for his or her treatment. If the person refuses any restitution, tell him you are going to donate money in his name to his favorite charity.

7. Finally, you need to complete your amends for your wrongful actions of the past by changing your actions in the future. This is especially important when making amends to those close to us who we've repeatedly harmed with our patterns of behavior. To these people we owe what is referred to in 12-step programs as "living amends." Our living amends are how we treat others from now on—far more important than any words we could say to them. To apologize for our past actions and then to go right back to hurting those we are close to would make our words empty indeed. Real improvement can be made in our ongoing relationships only by permanently changing our harmful attitudes and behaviors. This is the only true way to make up for the hurts of the past. The following example shows the importance of this last step:

Carlos, age 29: When I made my amends to my family, I knew I had to show them I'd really changed. They'd stood by me so many times, but I always let them down. They finally reached a point where they weren't willing to stand by me any longer. For years I'd lied to them, borrowed money I never repaid, and when my drug habit got really bad, I even stole from them. They told me they didn't want anything to do with me until I got help for my cocaine problem, so I didn't see them for over a year. When I finally lost everything, I got that help, but they still didn't believe I was going to stay clean. I wasn't too sure myself.

But I've been clean now for 8 months and I have a very strong program. When I reached the place in my recovery where I was finally ready and willing to make amends, I knew it wasn't going to be easy. I had to face how much I'd hurt my family and I had to show them I'd really changed.

I started out by apologizing for my behavior in the past. I spelled out exactly how I'd hurt each person in my family, just so they knew that I knew. Then I explained to them about my 12-step program, how I attended a meeting three times a week and how this helped me stay clean. I even told them there were no guarantees I'd stay clean, that I still battled urges and would probably battle them all my life. But I explained that the program wasn't just about not taking drugs—it was about working on the character defects that contributed to my drug problem in the first place—and that changing the way I relate to other people is just as important as being abstinent.

This is what really made the difference. They knew I'd been sorry for hurting them in the past—they knew I didn't really want to do some of the things I'd done, that I was out of control. They needed to know I had a handle on my problems somehow, that I was taking responsibility for finding out what was wrong with me and for changing my life. When they heard I was doing these things, they said it was a big relief for them. They could finally open the door a little and let me back into the family. They still don't trust me completely, but they treat me with a lot more respect than they had in the past. I know it's because they recognize I respect myself more, and for the first time in a long, long time, I'm being honest with myself and with them.

Get to the Root of Your Problem

If you have a lifetime pattern of similar behavior or your offense or offenses are something you've done often, you will need to do more than make amends. You will need to work on discovering the root of your problem. This is the only way you will be able to repair what is wrong inside of you and avoid repeating the behavior. This was the case with Charlene, as told by her friend Nancy:

> I never thought I'd speak to my friend, Charlene, again after what she did to me. [Nancy's friend, Charlene, had an affair with Nancy's husband.]
>
> You don't get over something like that very easily. I felt horribly betrayed by both of them, but for some reason it hurt even more to realize my so-called friend could do something like that to me. It almost ruined my marriage, but my husband convinced me that it had been Charlene who had come on to him. Not that that makes what he did okay, but I was able to understand a little better how he would be tempted. Charlene is a very beautiful, sexy woman and my husband and I weren't doing too well in the sex department. Charlene could have gotten any man she wanted and she usually did. Why did she have to go after my husband?
>
> Like I said, it almost broke up my marriage but not quite. It took me a long time to forgive my husband and we had to go to counseling over the whole thing. But now our marriage is actually better in some ways. I still don't completely trust him, but maybe that's better in some ways, too. I was a little too naive for my own good before.
>
> Things were just getting back to normal when Charlene called out of the blue. She begged me to hear her out, to let her explain why she'd done what she did. She sounded so sad—she was crying like a baby—that I finally gave in. I agreed to meet her at her apartment.
>
> She started out by telling me how sorry she was. She seemed very insecure and I believed she was sorry, but that didn't make me feel all that much better. I really needed to know why she'd done it. She told me that she'd been doing some real soul searching and that she'd gone to counseling to

find out what was wrong with her. She explained she'd been sexually abused by her father from the time she was 6 years old until she was 12. She'd always known this, but she never realized how much the abuse affected her. She said that she grew up believing that all men were like her father, and that doing whatever a man wanted sexually was the only way she could get the attention and approval she craved. That's why she'd been so promiscuous all her life. But there was even more to the story.

It turns out that she had a lot of anger stored up against her mother for allowing the abuse to occur. She said she was sure her mother knew because a few times she even walked in on them. Anyway, she had all this anger toward her mother and somehow it all came out on me. Here I had this husband and I seemed happy and she was jealous of that. She wanted to break us up because she didn't feel we had a right to be happy. Because she and I had gotten so close, she somehow got me all mixed up with her mother. It was like she was seeing her mother be happy when she didn't have a right to be. And she wanted me (really her mother) to face what her father was doing. It's all pretty complex stuff, but you get the idea.

Anyway, when she told me all this, she really broke down crying. She kept saying over and over how sorry she was and how she wouldn't have hurt me for the world. That I'd been the only person in her whole life who hadn't used her and the only person she'd ever trusted. She couldn't believe she'd betrayed my trust like that. I tell you, I was really touched. I couldn't help myself. I reached over to her and started holding her and we both burst out crying.

That afternoon we got close again. I knew she was really sorry, and because she couldn't really help what she'd done, I was able to forgive her. She'd had a horrible life and now I understood why she'd done what she'd done. The whole thing was so healing for both of us. After all, I'd forgiven my husband. Why couldn't I forgive her?

It doesn't mean I entirely trust her not to try to hurt me again in some way. But as long as she continues therapy, I feel pretty safe. Not that I trust Charlene and my husband together, mind you. I'm not that stupid. It's not that I really think either one of them would do it again, but I just don't believe in tempting fate. To tell you the truth, I can't even stand to see them together—it still hurts too much. But Charlene and I are closer than ever. I never imagined it could turn out this way.

By getting to the root of her problem, Charlene was able to make amends that really had substance. She didn't just tell her friend she was sorry; she explained why she did what she did (not as an excuse but because her friend wanted to understand). Because she promised to continue therapy, she gave Nancy the reassurance that she was not likely to repeat the same behavior, thus freeing Nancy to forgive her.

How to Apologize or Make Amends When You Have No Contact

There will be some people on your apology list with whom you have lost contact and you will need to make every effort possible to find them. But don't despair if you aren't immediately successful. Your willingness to find the person and to make amends is as important as your efforts. While you will need to continue searching, trust in the fact that you have begun the amends process.

Many of us wish we could apologize to those we have hurt in the past. Our unspoken apology lies heavy in our chest and we long to get it out. Unfortunately, there may be obstacles in our way. We may have lost contact with the person, or the person may have died.

Around the same time that my mother apologized to me, I discovered to my shock and horror that despite my efforts to the contrary, my worst nightmare had come true—I had become my mother. I was frozen with shame at this new awareness. As my life passed before me, I remembered many of the horrible things I'd said to friends and lovers—hurtful, spiteful, hateful things, words that had no doubt wounded them deeply. I remembered much of my inconsiderate, selfish, cruel behavior, which at the time seemed justified or acceptable. In the midst of this epiphany, I longed to apologize to these friends and lovers, but most were no longer in my life.

Of course, this was no coincidence. We hadn't merely lost track of one another. Some had fled from my life without warning and without a trace, and I had made it clear to others that I no longer wanted to know them. Now I wanted to go to each of them and pour out my heart. I wanted to tell them how sorry I was, how much I regretted my words and actions. I wanted to tell them that now I understood why they acted the way *they* did. That I didn't know I'd become a monster. I wanted to tell them that I wished I could take it back.

But I couldn't. And because I couldn't, I felt stuck and frustrated. I had to repeatedly replay in my mind what I had done. For a while this was good because I was continually reminded of my actions and was forced to make life changes. But after a while it was no longer healthy. I had to purge myself of my guilt and shame and self-loathing. I had to find a way to apologize to those I'd hurt even in their absence. And I had to find a way to forgive myself even if I didn't get a chance to ask for their forgiveness.

There are many other people who have a difficult time finding those they have harmed in order to make amends, particularly those in 12-step programs who are suddenly facing the truth about themselves and the effect their attitude and actions have had on others. The following strategies have worked for me and many of my clients. These strategies will help you find a way to apologize and rid yourself of your shame even if you no longer have contact with the people you hurt.

Making Indirect Amends

If you have tried to find someone you have offended and were unable to do so, you can still make amends. There are several ways to do this:

- Write down the words you would say if you were face-to-face. Include an acknowledgment of the wrong you did and of the effect you realize it had on the person's life, your actual apology (including words of regret), and the ways in which you plan to make restitution.

- If you have difficulty getting your words down on paper, try talking into a tape recorder, pretending that you are actually speaking to the person to whom you wish to make amends. Include all elements of the amends, just as if you were speaking in person.

- You can complete the restitution part of your amends by giving money to the person's family, donating money to the person's favorite charity, donating money to an appropriate service organization (e.g., a battered women's shelter, a drug or alcohol treatment center), volunteering for such an organization, or in some other appropriate way.

Continuing Your Search

While it is important to continue your search for those you've offended, these methods of indirect amends will help you to put the past behind you, and interestingly enough, they may open the door for the person you offended to come in. Many people in 12-step programs are surprised by the sudden, unexpected appearance of those they have on their amends list. This has been my experience as well. For instance, several years ago I lost contact with a close friend of over 20 years. I knew I owed her an apology but I no longer knew how to reach her. While writing this book I thought of her often and wished I could let her know how sorry I was for the way I had acted around her for several years.

During a book tour this past year, one of the reporters who interviewed me passed along a message. It turned out my long-lost friend worked with this reporter and had heard she was going to interview me. My friend sent a hello message and I sent a message back through the reporter, along with my business card. Even though my friend had moved to a different state, I truly believe that my willingness to apologize brought us back in contact. I'm happy to say that my friend was open to my apology and felt she owed me one in return for severing our relationship without an explanation. Although we have a long history together, in many ways we have started our friendship all over again.

You may wish to log on to my Web site **www.apologizing.com** for more information on how to find those with whom you've lost contact, as well as a way for you to reach out to those to whom you owe amends. By listing your name and e-mail address on the Web site, along with the name of the person to whom you wish to make amends, you have a greater chance of finding those with whom you've lost contact. If the person wishes to hear your amends, he or she can contact you by e-mail to make arrangements or to let you know he or she is willing to read your e-mail amends.

How to Make Amends When the Wronged Person Has Died

Some of the people on your apology list may have died, but this doesn't mean you have lost your opportunity to make amends. You can still make amends by doing the following:

- Write your amends down on paper or say the words into a tape recorder.

- Go to a place that reminds you of the person and read your letter out loud (or play your recording).

- Many people have found that once a person has died they feel a strong connection with the person's spirit and can talk directly to it. This can be especially poignant in a house of worship, in a candlelit room, or in another special place.

- As already suggested, you can make the restitution part of your amends by donating money to the wronged party's family or favorite charity, or by doing volunteer work for a nonprofit organization.

Making Amends to Yourself

Just as you need to make amends to others, you also need to make amends to yourself. Simply apply all that you've learned on how to make a meaningful apology and amends to yourself.

- Begin by making a list of all the things you have done to hurt or harm yourself. Include such things as how you may have abused your body, how you have sabotaged relationships or sabotaged success, and how you have deprived yourself of the things you've needed.

- You can make your actual amends to yourself by either writing a letter to yourself, by talking into a tape recorder, or by making a video.

- Once you have completed your amends, you will need to take them in. Allow a few days to pass and pick a time when you aren't distracted by anything else, and then revisit your amends, imagining that you are hearing them for the first time. Really take in your words, letting them heal the self-wounding, letting them wash over you like a healing salve.

CHAPTER 12

Healing Your Family When There Has Been an Estrangement

Children begin by loving their parents; as they grow older they judge them; sometimes they forgive them.

OSCAR WILDE

Everyone has unresolved issues with the past. Feelings of resentment, anger, and hurt involving our family of origin rank as one of the major issues that remain unresolved for most people. These feelings of anger and hurt are often transferred to our partners and our children, contaminating these relationships and preventing us from seeing our loved ones with any real clarity. In addition, many people have ongoing conflicts with their parents, siblings, or other family members that continue to plague them.

Apologizing to family members you have wronged, accepting the apologies of those who have wronged you, and asking for an apology from those who have wronged you can be the most effective tools in healing family conflicts and wounds, completing your unfinished business, and helping you to reunite with family members from whom you've become estranged.

Giving an Apology to an Estranged Family Member

If it was a family member's idea to stop seeing you, it will of course be up to you to apologize for the hurts, disappointments, betrayals, and slights that the person experienced because of your behavior. This was Glenda's situation:

> My sister and I stopped talking to each other over five years ago. Actually, she stopped talking to me because I refused to apologize to her for telling a secret she trusted me with. Looking back on it now, I realize it was my pride that was in the way. As I've gotten older, I've come to realize that my pride isn't as important as my sister. I miss her and want her back in my life. An apology now seems like a small price in order to make that happen.

The most important step family members can take in their efforts to reconcile is to apologize for their part in whatever it was that created the distance between themselves and their loved one. You will need to feel genuinely sorry for your part in the conflict and to be willing to admit what you did wrong. Otherwise, your reconciliation attempts will not be successful.

If Your Adult Child Has Stopped Seeing You

In Jerusalem, there is an ancient wall called the Western Wall. It is a sacred site for the Jewish people. Many years ago, people began leaving notes to God in the cracks and crevices of that 2,000-year-old wall, hoping that a special prayer would be answered.

In *How to Forgive When You Can't Forget*, Rabbi Charles Klein writes that when he makes his annual pilgrimage to Israel each year congregants often ask him to take along their prayers to insert in the wall. On one such trip a member of Klein's congregation opened his prayer and read the words out loud: "Dear God, You have given me so much in life. You have blessed me with health and with wealth. Please help my son to find a way to forgive me. I love him and I want him back. I miss him and I want him close again."

While I was touched deeply by this man's prayer, I couldn't help but think about how powerful this letter would be if sent directly to his son. And I couldn't help but wonder if he'd ever apologized directly to his son for whatever it was he had done.

Whatever your child's main complaint has been or whatever he or she has been asking of you in order to reconcile, the bottom line usually comes down to this—most adult children want their parent to admit what he or she did to hurt and damage them and to apologize. No matter how many other attempts you have made to reconcile with your child, if you haven't apologized to him or her for your past actions, these attempts have likely been futile ones. Even if your child tells you it is too late—that he or she has already tried to talk to you to no avail—if you are willing to apologize and then to listen to your child, I can almost guarantee that a reconciliation is not only possible but probable.

Often parents are keenly aware of what they need to apologize for. Their children may have already made it abundantly clear or the parents may already be aware that their behavior has been inappropriate, inconsiderate, or even abusive.

But in some cases parents are in the dark when it comes to discovering why their adult children have become estranged from them. If this describes your situation, you will need to put your pride aside and take a good hard look at yourself. When you look back on how you raised your child, on the ways that you treated her or him, both as a child and as an adult, do you have any regrets? Can you think of some things you may have done, or left undone, that might have hurt or damaged your child? The chances are that the behavior and situations that come to mind are the very things your adult child remembers and still feels hurt about.

You probably aren't totally in the dark as to your child's reasons for this estrangement. Chances are you have been aware that she has been unhappy with you or the relationship for quite some time, but you may have neglected to ask her what was wrong. She may have tried to tell you about how you have hurt her, or about behavior or attitudes of yours that offend her, but you may not have been willing to listen.

If you still feel stuck in terms of understanding why your child has become estranged from you, perhaps it will help you to review your own past and think about how you were treated as a child. If you were physically, verbally, or sexually abused, neglected, overly controlled, or criticized, the chances are high that you abused your own children in the same ways. Research shows that those who were abused as children are far more likely to become abusive parents than those who were not abused. There are basically four categories of child abuse:

1. *Physical abuse:* Physical abuse refers to any nonaccidental injury, including violent assault with an implement such as a belt, strap, switch, cord, brush, or paddle, resulting in bruises, welts, burns, broken bones, fractures, scars, or internal injuries. "Spanking" for purely disciplinary reasons is not generally regarded as child abuse, although if bruises result or if a tool is used it may be judged to be child abuse. Physical abuse also includes punching, slapping, pulling, yanking, choking, shaking, kicking, pinching, or torturing with tickling. It includes witnessing violence done to a parent or sibling.

2. *Physical neglect:* This includes abandonment; refusal to seek, allow, or provide treatment for illness or impairment; inadequate physical supervision; disregard of health hazards in the home; failure to provide adequate nutrition, clothing, or hygiene when services are available; keeping a child home from school repeatedly without cause; or failing to enroll a child in school.

3. *Emotional abuse:* Such abuse encompasses emotional or verbal assaults, including persistent teasing, belittling, or verbal attacks; close confinement such as tying a child up or locking him or her in a closet; inadequate nurturing such as that affecting failure-to-thrive babies; putting demands on a child that are beyond his or her capabilities; knowingly permitting antisocial behavior, such as delinquency; or ignoring a diagnosed emotional problem.

4. *Sexual abuse:* This abuse includes sexual molestation, incest, or exploitation for prostitution; the production of pornographic materials; or any other exploitation of a child for the sexual gratification of an adult. This can include physical sexual abuse, indirect sexual abuse, verbal sexual abuse, boundary violation, and emotional sexual abuse.

   • Physical sexual abuse includes sexual hugging or kissing, sexual fondling, oral or anal sex, intercourse, masturbation of the victim, or forcing the victim to masturbate the offender.

- Indirect sexual abuse includes any act of voyeurism or exhibitionism on the part of an adult toward a child for the conscious or unconscious sexual stimulation of the adult. With voyeurism, the adult becomes sexually stimulated by watching a child dress, undress, take a bath or shower, or use the toilet.
- Exhibitionism is when an adult exposes his genitals to a child or walks around naked for the purpose of being sexually stimulated.
- Verbal sexual abuse includes using inappropriate sexual words or obscenities in an abusive way toward a child, asking inappropriate questions about a child's sexual life or sexual anatomy, talking about sex in front of a child whose age level is inappropriate, or making remarks about the sexual parts of a child's body (e.g., remarks about the size of a child's breasts or penis).
- Boundary violation includes exposure of children to their parents' sexual behavior or naked bodies. It also includes denying privacy to a child, such as walking in on the child in the bathroom or in his or her bedroom.
- Emotional sexual abuse occurs when one or both parents bond inappropriately with one of their children. When a parent uses a child to meet his or her emotional needs, the relationship can easily become sexualized and romanticized. Emotional sexual abuse also occurs when one parent has a relationship with the child that is more important than the relationship the parent has with his or her spouse.

Often parents don't realize that their behavior toward their children was actually abusive. This is especially true of those who were abused themselves as children in any of the above ways. You may have been treating your children the way you were treated without even realizing you were harming them. Times have changed, and some practices that were once accepted as appropriate in terms of child rearing and punishment have now been found to be not only inappropriate but harmful. If you now realize that you were abused and passed on this legacy of abuse to your children, it is very important that you explain this to your children and apologize for your behavior.

Many parents have problems with this concept because they feel they are blaming their own parents. But facing and telling the truth about the legacy of abuse is not the same as blaming your own parents for your behavior. There is a big difference between blaming and taking responsibility. Blaming is a negative action—an attempt at avoiding responsibility by placing fault on someone else. Taking responsibility is a positive action, even when it is accompanied by an explanation as to why the actions were taken. By explaining to your children why you were abusive, you are not avoiding responsibility; you are telling them the truth about their family and letting them know that it was not your intention to harm them.

As I explained earlier, my mother was finally able to apologize for the emotional abuse she had inflicted on me as a child and as an adult. Once she realized that her behavior had been abusive, she felt terrible about herself. I had wanted an apology and recognition on my mother's part as to how her behavior had affected me, but I didn't want her to continue feeling bad about herself. I knew, from my many years of working as a psychotherapist, especially from my work with survivors of abuse, that my mother more than likely had been emotionally abused herself as a child.

When I explained this to her, she adamantly denied having received any such treatment. She had always raved about how wonderful her mother had been, what a loving, gregarious, and magnanimous person she was. In fact, she often compared me with my grandmother (who had died before I was born).

I let it go for the time being but brought up the issue several other times in the following few years. But it wasn't until my mother was close to death that she finally told me the truth. She had felt too loyal to her mother to tell me before. She explained that her mother had been an alcoholic and that when she drank she would become belligerent and hypercritical (just as she herself did when she was drinking). She even told me that her mother had been drunk the day she was killed (I'd always known that my grandmother had been hit by a car). It was very painful for my mother to finally tell me the truth—that my grandmother had been drinking and had decided to walk down the road at night to see a friend and was hit by a car, probably because she was in the middle of the street.

Although it was painful for her to tell me the truth about her mother, I knew it was also liberating. At first she felt as if she were being disloyal to her mother, who she loved very much, but later on she told me it had helped her to come to a place of acceptance about her own behavior toward me and even about her mother's behavior toward her.

As for me, it was like finding another missing piece to the puzzle about my family. I now added emotional abuse to the myriad of things that added up to my family legacy—alcoholism, arrogance, charisma, artistic talent, judgmentalism, intellect, gregariousness. Like all families, our legacy was made up of good and bad traits. Some I am grateful for; others I have to work to overcome.

Listen and Learn

If you still don't know why your child has become estranged from you, you will need to ask for the reason and then be willing to really listen. If you feel you have already listened, you will need to do so in a different way. Perhaps you need to just listen and not talk back—not defend yourself, not argue, not correct what you think are inaccuracies.

It is difficult to sit quietly and listen to people tell you about all the bad things you have done, remind you of your shortcomings, or blame you for their unhappiness and their problems. But if you want your child back in your life, this is exactly what you must be willing to do.

Bringing the Family Back Together When Childhood Abuse Has Occurred

Many, many families have been torn apart because of childhood abuse. Because of their denial, fear of the truth, pride, need to be right, guilt, anger, and downright stubbornness, family members have turned away from one another at a time when they need each other the most. Because of their own pain, family members have said things to one another that they never imagined they would say, done things to each other that they never imagined they could do. Family members have stopped speaking to and seeing one another, and have even disowned one another over the issue of child abuse.

Family members have turned against one another, refusing to admit when they are wrong, refusing to listen, refusing to even be open to the possibility that they might have been blind to the abuse.

For Nonabusive Parents, Siblings, and Other Family Members

Many times, survivors feel compelled to separate either temporarily or permanently from family members who they feel do not believe them or who are not supportive of them regarding the abuse. Even if your loved one has chosen to take this step with you, there is still hope for reconciliation. If you are truly willing to open your mind and heart to the survivor and what she or he has been through, if you are willing to swallow your pride and to admit that you acted either too defensively or too protectively toward the wrongdoer, if you are willing to listen now or in a way that you could not before, then you probably can look forward to a fresh start with your loved one.

The first thing you will need to do is open your mind and heart to your loved one. The fact that you are reading this chapter indicates that you have already done so to some degree. Perhaps you are more educated now about the issue of abuse, having heard more about it through the media, by listening to friends talk, or by reading books. Perhaps one or more of your friends have even told you about their experience with abuse, either personally or through their children. Or perhaps your own memories are starting to surface and you either suspect or are now certain that you too were a victim. Last, but certainly not least, perhaps you believe your loved one now because someone else in the family has confided in you that he or she was also abused by the same person, or it has been discovered that some other child in the family was abused by the same person. For whatever reason, if you are now more willing to believe what your loved one was trying to tell you, then this is wonderful news for both the survivor and for you. Even though it is painful, facing the truth truly does set you free and may help you to get your child, your sibling, your grandchild, or your niece or nephew back.

The next thing you will need to do is swallow your pride. If a family member has stopped seeing you, you may have already come to the conclusion that you miss and need him more than you need your pride. As difficult as it may be for you to be the one to [reach] out, this is what you will need to do. Your loved one probably fee[ls] too afraid, too hurt, and too hopeless to reach out to you. He probably tried for a long time to get you to believe his story, or to get you to understand just how damaged he was because of the abuse, yet you were unable or unwilling to do so. He probably came to the conclusion, as many survivors do, that he needed to be away from you in order to recover from the abuse because your disbelief caused him to doubt himself and his perceptions too much. And so he is now probably unable or unwilling to reach out to you, even if he sometimes wants to. He probably believes that it is a lost cause and he doesn't feel it is healthy for him to subject himself to any more disappointment or pain from you.

You will have to be the one to initiate reconciliation. The most important step you can take will be to apologize to the survivor. You will also need to show your loved one that you are sincere and have changed. This means doing things differently than you are probably used to doing them. Perhaps it means admitting right away that you were wrong.

You will probably need to be more direct than you are used to being when you call or write. Tell your loved one the purpose of your communication right away (e.g., "I have been thinking about what you told me and I now feel I am more open to believing you. I would like to talk to you further about it"). If you feel remorse for not believing him earlier, say, "I know I was wrong for not believing you before." And most importantly, state your intentions: "I am willing to listen with an open mind," or, "I want to support you now in any way I can."

If your loved one agrees to talk to you again, you will need to be prepared to listen in a way that you never have before. When we truly listen to others, we are focusing all our attention on what they are saying, not on what we want to say in response or thinking of a way to defend ourselves. We do not interrupt but listen attentively until the other person has finished saying what he or she needs to say.

While you are listening to your loved one, try to hear exactly what he or she is saying. Don't jump to conclusions and don't make assumptions—just hear the words. For example, you may imagine that he or she is blaming you for the abuse in some way—blaming you for not knowing it was going on, for not stopping it, or for exposing him or her to the abuser—when in reality he or she is doing no such thing. Often when we feel guilty about something, when we blame ourselves for something, we hear blame from other people when it isn't even there. If you tend to do this, it can cause you to be defensive, to close down, and to be unable to truly hear your loved one or to be able to be supportive of her or him. Whether your loved one blames you for some aspect of the abuse is really irrelevant at this point anyway. What is important is what happened to him or her, how it made your loved one feel, how it affected his or her life, and how he or she feels today. Don't let your own tendency to be defensive get in your way of truly listening and being supportive.

If You Abused a Family Member

If you abused your child, grandchild, niece, sister, cousin, or some other family member, you will need to do more than apologize and listen to his or her feelings about what you did. You will need to take responsibility for your actions in all of the following ways:

1. Admit to yourself that what you did was wrong regardless of what led you to do it.

2. Admit to the victim that you abused him or her.

3. Take utter and complete responsibility for the abuse.

4. Be willing to listen to the victim while he or she tells you how your behavior has affected his or her life.

5. Apologize to the survivor for the damage you caused.

6. Admit the abuse to other family members.

7. Learn from your mistake so that you will not repeat it. Get therapy if you need it to stop hurting others. Make a commitment to yourself to never hurt someone like that again.

8. Do whatever is necessary to repair the harm you caused.

Since words are often not enough, sometimes you need to offer to repair the damage you did by offering restitution in the form of financial assistance to help the survivor pay for therapy or a promise that you will enter therapy yourself.

For more help for the families of survivors of childhood sexual abuse, please refer to my book, *Families in Recovery*.

Receiving an Apology from
an Estranged Family Member

For many, receiving an apology from an estranged family member can feel like a wonderful gift, as it did in my case. But for others, it may be a gift that is unappreciated or an obligation that has been fulfilled far too late. Some have worked so hard to defend themselves that one "I'm sorry" isn't going to penetrate their self-imposed wall of protection. It may just seem like too little too late.

However, you should never minimize or negate a genuine apology. While you may or may not choose to forgive or to reconcile with a family member who has hurt you, you owe it to yourself to be as open as possible to receiving his or her apology. To do otherwise is to rob yourself of an incredible healing experience.

If you are having difficulty developing the empathy that is necessary in order to forgive, remember that the person who wronged you is a fallible, vulnerable, even needy human being who is prone to failure, pettiness, and selfishness as we all are. Often we hold others to a much higher standard than we do ourselves. This is especially true of our parents and other caretakers. For example, as children we perceived our parents as being all-knowing and larger than life. They were supposed to practice what they preached and always do the right thing. But the reality of the situation was that our parents weren't always good role models and they often made the very mistakes they tried to help us avoid. They didn't always do the right thing and they often fell short of being good parents.

Many children grow up enraged with their parents for their shortcomings, mistakes, or mistreatment. And, unfortunately, many adult children are still unwilling to accept their parents' vulnerabilities and shortcomings as a fact of life. To them, their parents were supposed to be above all that, to be better than other people. Because they can't accept the fact that their parents were just like everyone else, they can't forgive.

If you are having a difficult time accepting an apology from a family member, it is important that you examine the reasons for your resistance. Refer to Chapter 5 and reread the information on learning how to accept an apology. If you would like to work toward forgiveness but are unable to, refer to Chapter 6 on the seven obstacles to accepting an apology. Once you've identified the obstacles that are in your way, you can begin to work on overcoming them. The following exercise will also help you overcome your resistance.

EXERCISE

Examine Your Resistance to the Apology

Ask yourself the following questions:

A. *Do you really believe that the other person is genuinely sorry? If not, why not?* Write about the reasons why you think the other person is simply going through the motions, lying, or trying to manipulate you.

B. *Why are you afraid to accept this person's apology? Are you afraid he or she will hurt you in the same or in similar ways all over again?* If you answered yes, write about your fears and the ways that you can protect yourself better from this person. There are no guarantees that the other person might not slip back and do the very same things, but you do have the power to change the way you interact with him or her. Protecting yourself from future harm will be your responsibility, not the other person's. On the other hand, it is difficult to trust someone who has hurt you, and it is up to the other person to win back your trust. List some ways that he or she may do this.

C. *Do you feel that the other person was pressured by other family members or by circumstances to apologize instead of the apology coming from a genuine place of remorse?* Write about these feelings and what motives you think drove this person to apologize. It's perfectly acceptable for you to ask the other person what his or her motives actually were for apologizing. Whatever the reason, recognize the fact that she did humble herself before you when she made the apology. It takes courage to admit you are wrong, even if you are pressured into doing so.

Don't allow other family members to pressure you into accepting an apology or forgiving before you are ready. And remember that you can forgive a person spiritually without reconciling with that person. You may be willing to forgive what he or she did in the past but unwilling to risk being hurt in the future. If accepting an apology or forgiving feels like you are leaving yourself or your children wide open for future mistreatment, as in cases of childhood abuse, by all means don't accept the apology.

Asking for an Apology from an Estranged Family Member

If the estrangement was your idea and your relative has not stepped forward to apologize, you will need to ask for an apology. Just make sure you are willing to forgive before you ask and that you have found a way of releasing most of your anger in a constructive way. Otherwise, you will sabotage your efforts. Refer to Chapter 8 for more general advice on how to go about asking for your apology.

Asking an Estranged Parent for an Apology

Deep inside, most adult children who are estranged from their parent(s) have a secret dream of getting back together and working things out. Even though they knew at the time that divorce or separation was the healthiest choice they could make, after some time apart many adult children know they still love their parent and long for a reconciliation. As time passes, as old wounds heal, it is natural to feel more forgiving of even the cruelest parents and to miss even the most unlovable ones. This is what a client, Cynthia, shared with me:

> I didn't stop seeing my father to punish or manipulate him, but to make a statement that I would no longer allow him to abuse me verbally and emotionally.
>
> I didn't see him for over 3 years, and a lot happened to me in that time. Because I wasn't around his abusiveness and because of therapy, my self-esteem improved greatly. I married a wonderful man and we have two children. For the first time in my life I felt good about myself and my life, and I wanted to share some of it with my dad, if he wasn't still abusive, that is. I wanted him to meet my husband and kids, and I guess there was also a part of me that wanted him to see that I was successful and had turned out well, not because of him but in spite of him.

I decided that I was now strong enough to ask him for an apology for the way he had treated me. Much to my surprise, it wasn't as difficult as I'd anticipated it would be. We met at a coffee shop because I wanted to meet at a neutral place. As soon as we sat down I told him that I felt he had been emotionally abusive toward me and how it had affected me. At first he bristled and I thought for a moment that he was going to get up and leave. But then he looked at me and said, "I was too hard on you at times. I know that. But I did it for your own good. I didn't mean to hurt your feelings or make you feel insecure like you say it did."

I started to interrupt him, to tell him that it didn't just feel like he criticized and yelled at me for "my own good" but because he had become enraged with me for not minding him. But then he said, "I guess I lost my temper with you too. I didn't mean to. I just fly off the handle sometimes. I know it's a problem and I've been working on it. I'm sorry for that. I really am."

This was all I could have hoped for from my father—an admission and an apology. I now felt that I could be safe with him, that since he'd admitted he had a problem with his anger and was actually working on it, it wasn't as likely that he'd become abusive with me again. And after having the courage to confront him, I now felt strong enough to stand up for myself if he did become abusive again.

Like Cynthia, some adult children discover that being away from their parent has made them much healthier and stronger—so much so that they find they can now take much better care of themselves in the presence of their parent. Cynthia gave the relationship with her father one more try. The last time I saw her, she reported: "I am no longer a child around my father. I no longer feel like his victim but his equal. Whenever he starts to bristle, I give him a look that says 'Don't mess with me,' and he backs down. It's amazing."

Reconciliation Is Not the Same as Forgiveness

It is not necessary for you to have completed the forgiveness process in order to reconcile with your parent or other family member.

Perhaps during the reconciliation process itself, you may obtain enough trust and healing to be able to forgive.

Some people never forgive even though they reconcile with their loved one. "How can this be," you might ask. "If I don't forgive, how can I possibly reconcile?" If you can really accept the fact that everyone is both good and bad, it is possible to love someone for their good qualities in spite of what they have done to hurt you. And some people are able to reconcile even though they can't completely forgive because they can forgive the person even though they can't forgive the act.

It is up to you to decide about forgiveness or reconciliation. You will know if the time is right. Trust your instincts, follow your heart, and do not allow circumstances or other people to pressure you into a decision prematurely.

Giving, accepting, and asking for apologies from estranged family members can be a giant step toward reconciliation. If a family member has stopped having contact with you, there is probably a very good reason. More than likely you know what it is if you are really honest with yourself. However, if you really do not know the reason for the estrangement, be open to hearing your estranged relative when he or she tries to tell you. Then be honest with yourself and be willing to admit when you have been wrong. This will help you gain the respect of your relative as well as respect for yourself.

If you receive an apology from a relative who has wronged you, give him or her the courtesy of listening to it with an open heart. Respect the courage it took to give the apology and allow the words to heal you of the bitterness that has poisoned your soul. Then give yourself time to decide whether you are willing or able to reconcile.

If you have been estranged from a family member but now feel you are more able or willing to be around him or her, you have nothing to lose by asking for an apology. It is very possible that with the time and distance that has existed between you, your relative is now more willing to admit his or her wrongdoing. And if he or she isn't, this information will help you determine whether you are now willing to reconcile.

CHAPTER 13

Healing Your Marriage or Romantic Relationship

Would you rather be right or be loved?

SANDRA RAY

A happy marriage is the union of two good forgivers.

ROBERT QUILLEN

Aside from the words *I love you*, the words *I'm sorry* are probably the most powerful words anyone can ever say to another person. In fact, in many cases, saying "I'm sorry" also says "I love you": *I love you enough to set aside my pride. I love you enough to admit I was wrong. I care about your feelings and feel bad that I hurt you. I love you enough to get some help so that I won't do it again.* Admitting a fault or apologizing for hurting your partner's feelings not only shows love but strength and commitment.

Apologizing shows strength because it often takes courage to admit when we are wrong. It's far easier to deny wrongdoing than to admit a mistake and to face the consequences. It is the more insecure person who must always be right, the courageous one who can humble himself or herself and be wrong.

Apologizing shows commitment when you place your relationship and your partner's feelings ahead of your pride and are able to say, "It's more important to me to have your love than to be right" or, "I love you so much that I am willing to work on my faults and correct my mistakes so that we can be together."

Unfortunately, many couples don't apologize often enough and some never do. One or both may allow their pride to get in the way even when they know they are wrong. This is especially true when one or both partners are extremely competitive or when there is a power struggle occurring in the relationship.

It is also common for individuals to be oblivious to the hurt they cause their partner, either because they are so focused on how their partner hurts them or because they are simply too preoccupied to notice how their behavior affects other people. These hurts build up and create tension, conflict, and distance between partners.

There is a deep wounding that occurs when a person we care for refuses to apologize. In time, this wounding can cause us to close down emotionally, to become emotionally distant, angry, or bitter.

The purpose of this chapter is to show you how apology can heal many relationship problems, as well as inspire and help sustain respect, trust, and caring. In addition, I discuss the differences between men and women regarding apology, and provide separate advice to women and men on how apology can help a relationship to thrive.

When One Apologizes and the Other Doesn't

A good relationship is based on respect, trust, and caring. If one partner cannot apologize to the other, not only does it show a lack of respect and caring toward his or her partner, but it makes it difficult to continue to respect and trust the person who can't apologize.

Often it is the case that one person in a relationship readily apologizes for his or her behavior while the other one doesn't. Stereotypically, we think of it as a male/female issue, and in many respects it can be. In most cultures, males are discouraged from apologizing whereas females are encouraged to do so, often to an extreme. Women, far more than men, grow up being taught to apologize as a matter of courtesy. In addition, women are raised to be pleasers and to take care of the feelings of others far more than men, and apologizing often becomes a way to do this. Finally, women are biologically hardwired to value connection, compromise, and cooperation more than men. Apologizing becomes a natural way for women to express and practice these three important values.

Earlier in the book I explained why some people have a more difficult time apologizing than others. Understanding why some people have difficulty apologizing can engender more tolerance and compassion in a relationship. This is especially true when it comes to women understanding the reasons why many men have difficulty apologizing. Therefore, I suggest that in addition to reading those sections specifically addressed to you, women also read the sections I have written for men in order to better understand their partner. The same holds true for men. Understanding why some women apologize too often and that they probably need to begin *asking* for an apology will not only help you understand your partner better but help equalize the relationship.

I don't want to give the impression that all men have difficulty apologizing and that all women apologize too often, however. Sometimes it is the reverse. There are many women to whom apologizing is difficult and there are some men who tend to apologize too often or inappropriately. If this is the situation in your relationship, just follow the advice that is appropriate to your circumstances even if it is addressed to the opposite sex.

Advice to Men

One of the biggest complaints men have about their partners is that women tend to nag and complain too much. Ironically, one of the biggest complaints women have about men is that they don't listen. In their defense, women explain that the reason they nag is that they don't feel heard.

If men simply *acknowledge* what their partner has said, she might not feel compelled to repeat herself. For example, if you simply say, "I hear you" when she asks you to do something, or, "I know you feel that way" when she explains how your behavior affected her, she will at least feel heard, which is very important, particularly to women.

But you can go a step further. When your partner complains to you that you haven't done something, *apologize* to her. Apologizing for your oversights will not only let your partner know you have heard her, it will let her know that you are sorry for your actions or inaction.

Apology is very important to women. This is partly because fairness and equality are so important to them. Fairness goes hand in hand with cooperation and with meeting the needs of all within a group. Equality is important because most women have had to fight hard to achieve it. And because most women have an easier time admitting when they are wrong than most men, they have a difficult time understanding what the big deal is for a man. They view a man who has difficulty apologizing as stubborn, unfair, and ultimately uncaring.

If you have difficulty apologizing, you can train yourself to do so by following these suggestions:

1. If you have a tendency to make excuses for your oversights or inappropriate behavior, try catching yourself in the act. As soon as you notice that you are making excuses, say, "But it doesn't really matter why I did it. The point is I did it and I'm sorry."

2. If you were not raised to apologize for oversights (such as forgetting an anniversary), it will be difficult to train yourself to do it now, but you can. You'll probably need to take your cue from your partner at first. If she tells you she's hurt because you forgot your anniversary, apologize. Don't make excuses; don't lie and say you planned a surprise. And don't be silent and secretly plan to make it up to her later. Just apologize.

3. Most women tend to be more sensitive emotionally than men, and men often have difficulty understanding why women get their feelings hurt so often for seemingly minor incidents. But the point is that if your partner's feelings were hurt by something you did or didn't do, she deserves an apology. If your partner tells you she is hurt by your behavior, apologize. Don't make excuses and don't tell her she shouldn't feel hurt. Don't tell her she's being silly or being overly sensitive. And most especially, don't tell her she's immature or acting like a baby. Just apologize.

4. Men often feel that if they didn't do something intentionally, they don't need to apologize. But apologizing doesn't mean you

are admitting you intended to hurt someone and it doesn't mean you are a bad person. In fact, when you apologize it is usually understood that you did not intend to hurt the other person's feelings. You are simply apologizing for the fact that the other person's feelings were indeed hurt, and that is usually all a woman wants to know.

5. If you find it difficult to say the words *I'm sorry*, buy a card and write the words down or write your partner a note of apology.

6. If you haven't been able to keep a promise, apologize and then renegotiate the agreement. Don't just ignore the fact that you've broken your promise because this will cause your partner to build up resentment toward you. And don't make excuses for why you didn't keep your promise. Just apologize for breaking it and make a new agreement that is more workable.

7. If your partner tends to apologize in order to keep the peace, help her by reminding her she doesn't have to do this. If she starts to apologize for something she isn't responsible for, say, "You didn't do anything wrong, so there's no need to say you're sorry. I'm the one who needs to apologize."

Advice to Women

While women need to apologize too, many women tend to over-apologize or to apologize inappropriately. This tendency plays an equal role in creating problems in relationships. By apologizing too often, taking responsibility for more than their share of the problems in the relationship, and failing to ask for an apology when they are offended, women invite mistreatment. This behavior also leads to harboring grudges and distancing themselves from their partner, including withdrawing sexually.

As mentioned earlier, most women are raised to be polite and to always apologize if they have offended someone. In addition, women are raised to be pleasers and caretakers, and they often take care of others by apologizing profusely when there is a disagreement. More than willing to take responsibility for their part in a dispute, women apologize easily and often. And since women are biologically conditioned to value compromise, connection, and cooperation, they often apologize in their efforts to keep the peace.

But women also tend to *overapologize*. They apologize automatically, even when they aren't the ones who made the mistake. They apologize as a way of saying *I care about you and don't want you to hurt.* They apologize as a way of maintaining peace in a relationship, even when they are still hurt or angry at the other person. They even apologize and take the blame for something they didn't do just to appease another person.

Unfortunately, when you overapologize, especially when it is extreme, you convey weakness, which invites others to take advantage of your vulnerability. When you constantly apologize just to keep the peace, you send the message that you will do anything, accept any blame, just to keep a man or maintain a relationship.

And when you don't ask for an apology when you have a right to one, you send the message to your partner that he can continue the same behavior. You may also begin to resent your partner for not apologizing on his own. The resentment builds over time, causing you to distance yourself, disrespect your partner, and eventually your loving feelings are eroded entirely.

In order to break these patterns, you may need to retrain yourself in the following ways:

1. Start noticing how often you apologize. Notice how many times the words *I'm sorry, Forgive me,* or *It was my fault* come out of your mouth.

2. If you notice you are apologizing a lot, think about why you're doing so. Is it an automatic response? Is it your way of avoiding conflict? Or is it due to low self-esteem?

3. The next time you catch yourself apologizing, take a deep breath and wait a few minutes. Depending on the situation, ask yourself the following questions:

   - Why am I apologizing?
   - Did I really do anything I should feel sorry about or was I just being myself?
   - Was it my fault or am I just trying to keep the peace?
   - Am I really sorry for what I did or am I still angry?
   - Did I intend to do what I did? (Sometimes it's perfectly normal to want to hurt someone's feelings, especially if that person has hurt yours, and it's perfectly normal *not* to feel sorry about it.)

    ● What am I trying to accomplish with my apology? Is this the best way to accomplish it?

4. If your partner tends to make gestures such as buying flowers instead of apologizing to you verbally and directly, the next time he does this acknowledge the gesture but name it for what it is. You might say, "Thank you for the flowers. Is this your way of saying you're sorry for last night?" This will bring things out in the open and encourage him to apologize more directly in the future. And your question may force him to say "yes," or at least nod his head in agreement, which is at least a beginning.

Power Struggles

Often the reason one or both partners in a relationship refuse to apologize is because it feels to them like a relinquishing of power. Both partners are afraid, hurt, and angry, but no one wants to make the first conciliatory move for fear of losing ground. It becomes a standoff.

How do you go about breaking the stalemate? Since in this society women still tend to be more comfortable with their feelings than men, women are probably going to have to be the first ones to make a move, at least in the beginning.

It is important to understand and to remember that if a man feels attacked he's going to feel vulnerable, and therefore he isn't as likely to admit he's wrong. Ask yourself if your voice or posture appears to be attacking. If so, think of a way to approach your partner in a manner that's not so threatening. One way is to talk about yourself, such as saying, "I feel hurt when you are insensitive to my needs," instead of saying, "You're an insensitive jerk."

If your partner appears calm enough to listen, try explaining why you feel hurt, again without going on the attack. For example, try saying, "It hurts me when you call me irrational. It's a low blow, and just because I don't agree with you, it doesn't mean I'm irrational."

Remember my friend whose partner told her she reminded him of her mother? Instead of telling him how she felt, she attacked him: "When you tell me I'm like my mother, it's such a joke. You're the one with mother problems, buster." This just threw gasoline on the fire and started the argument all over again.

When she told me about their argument over lunch, I asked her how his comment about her becoming like her mother had made her feel. "It scares me when he says that because my biggest fear is of becoming like her. He knows this, and it hurts that he'd use that information against me like that. I feel afraid to trust him with any further information about myself in the future."

I suggested she apologize to him for attacking him and then try telling him exactly what she had told me—how his comment about her mother caused her to feel hurt and afraid. The next time I saw her, she reported that she'd done just that and it had worked.

"I couldn't believe it. After I finished telling him how I felt, he said, 'I didn't realize you were so sensitive about your mother. Now I can see why my comment made you so angry. Don't worry, I won't say anything like that again.'"

Of course, asking women to make the first move is putting a big burden on them. Men need to take responsibility for working past their resistance to apology and for being able to put their pride aside for the sake of the relationship. This, of course, is a tall order and it takes time to overcome years of conditioning.

In the meantime, many couples have found that actions speak louder than words. Here's a summary of ways that some men have found to apologize until they can finally find the courage to say "I'm sorry."

Josh, age 24: When Samantha and I argue, she usually admits when she is wrong. But I have a hard time doing that. So instead I do other things that let her know I'm sorry, like buying her flowers or leaving "I love you" notes around the house.

Alex, age 52: In all the years we've been married, I've never been able to say "I'm sorry." What I do instead is to be especially nice to Paula for the next several weeks after an argument. I help her clean up the dishes after dinner and I'll do the laundry and wash the car. I figure she'll know how sorry I am by how much I help out around the house.

Eric, age 36: Saying "I'm sorry" is impossible for me. My way of apologizing after a bad night of arguing is to get up early and make breakfast the next morning and bring it to Nancy in bed.

What Do We Need to Apologize For?

While both women and men feel they are guilty of impatience, rudeness, being inconsiderate, not paying enough attention to their partner, misjudging or distrusting one another, not having enough empathy toward their partner (being unwilling to see their partner's point of view), and taking their partner for granted, I've found that women and men tend to feel they also have different things to apologize for.

Why Men Need to Apologize to Women

Many men don't even try to get past their resistance to apologizing. They simply write off their partner's complaints as nagging and never being pleased. Their perception of women in general is that they are overly sensitive, petty, and have expectations of men that are far too high.

Other men realize they actually do have many reasons to apologize. Among other things, men need to apologize to women for the following:

- Being insensitive to their partner's needs
- Being so self-focused that they neglect to zero in on how their partner is feeling or what is going on in her life
- Not really listening to what their partner is saying
- Not saying things diplomatically enough (being too direct or rude)
- Being critical

Why Women Need to Apologize to Men

While women can and must teach men how to empathize and how to be more sensitive to their needs, they need to be careful that they don't fall into the trap of trying to change men. This is what co-dependency is all about. And no one, especially men, wants to feel as if they are being "trained." The best women can do is show men, by example, how to be more vulnerable, trusting, and empathetic. Men often complain that they feel their partner treats them as if they were a project, and, in fact, this is what many women do. They enter a relationship convinced they can change a man instead of accepting him for who he is. This is very unfair. If you don't love a man just the way he is, you shouldn't be with him.

In addition to the above, women need to apologize to men for the following:

- Giving them double messages—for example, be more sensitive and more emotional, but don't be too much of a wimp because women want men to be strong
- Assuming that all men are the same—for example, all men have difficulty making a commitment
- Not trusting their partner
- Not being more patient (especially for their husband's lack of emotionality and vulnerability)
- Expecting their partner to always be the strong one, to always make the first move romantically and sexually

EXERCISE

Discover Who Owes Whom an Apology

A. List all the things you feel your partner owes you an apology for. Include all the things he or she has done that have hurt or angered you, going back as far as you can.

B. Now list all the things you feel you owe your partner an apology for, going back as far as you can in your memory.

   It may take some time to complete either or both lists. You can do so over a period of a few hours or days, coming back to your list as you think of more items.

C. After you have completed both lists, pay attention to how you now feel about the items you listed in part A. Do you feel even stronger that your partner owes you an apology for all those items on your list, or has putting down your grievances on paper caused your anger to subside a little?

D. Now compare how you feel about the items you listed in part A after making your own list in part B. Do you feel a little less angry and judgmental about what your partner has done to you after listing the things you've done to your partner, or is the reverse true? After making your list in part B, do you feel even more angry at your partner?

If the latter is true, I'd like you to make still another list: Which of the items in part A have you been guilty of doing to your partner?

E. Now go back to your list in part A and decide which of the items you feel are the most important and put a check mark beside each. Of these items, which do you still wish to ask your partner for an apology for?

Throughout the years, I've found that by asking couples who come into therapy to complete exercises such as the one above, I can help them to identify problems right away and to open up the lines of communication, as well as help them to move past resentments they've held for years and to move toward forgiveness.

When Loving No Longer Feels Safe

There is no doubt that many of today's couples suffer from a strong sense of disconnection. Part of the reason is that the relationship no longer feels safe for either partner. You have to feel safe in order to express your deepest feelings. You have to feel safe in order to be emotionally vulnerable. In order to risk true intimacy, which is the act of letting someone else enter our private world of thoughts, emotions, dreams, and fears, we must trust that it is safe to do so.

No one can feel safe with someone who repeatedly hurts them. Most especially, no one can feel safe when the person who hurt them doesn't apologize.

Most of us tend to be more vulnerable with our partners than with any other human being. We care more about what our partner thinks about us, and our partner usually knows more about us than anyone else.

When we first fall in love, most of us open up to our lovers and share our most intimate secrets, desires, and feelings. We have an intense need for our lover to really know who we are and we have an equally intense desire get to know our partner. We listen closely as our new partner tells us about his past, wanting desperately to understand why he is who he is. We encourage our new partner to express her feelings and we comfort and sympathize when she shares her pain, fears, and anger. We take it all in without judgment. We love him and so we love everything about him, including his frailties and shortcomings. The message we send our new partner by our words and our deeds is *You are safe with me. You can trust me with your feelings and your secrets. I won't judge you. I love you for who you are.*

We can relay this message to our new partner because our hearts are open. The state of being in love has allowed us to be far more loving and understanding and far less judgmental than we have been at any other time in our lives. Our partner senses our openness and feels incredibly safe. In this atmosphere of safety comes great healing. Not only are we able to share with one another stories and secrets that we have never been able to share with anyone, helping to heal our past, but we are able to share our fears—making them less frightening in the process. And when we share our dreams and hopes for the future with our partner, we come to feel that they can, in fact, be realized.

But all this tends to change as we enter more deeply into the relationship. Now the person who was our source of comfort and encouragement becomes the source of great pain and disappointment. Since our hearts are so open, we are easily hurt. In the day-to-day workings of a relationship, our feelings can be hurt often. If we are both aware of this and sensitive to our partner's feelings, these hurts can be soothed by words of regret and promises that we will not repeat the hurtful acts. But if one or both partners become defensive, insist on always being right, or refuse to apologize, our wounds not only go unsoothed but become even more raw.

The more raw our wounds become, the more sensitive we become to future hurts. In time, most of us have no other choice but to protect our wounds and ourselves by beginning to close our hearts. We are no longer willing to be as vulnerable and open to our partner. We stop sharing our true feelings.

Because we are so hurt, we begin to be more judgmental of our partner. We become impatient with the very faults and shortcomings we once accepted. Soon the relationship is no longer safe for either partner. We are no longer being healed by our love, but instead are constantly hurt by it. We are no longer growing together but are growing apart.

Apology can change all of this. Apology can help you return to a state of acceptance and understanding. It can help you reenter that magical cocoon of safety, compassion, and forgiveness you once shared together. Ultimately, it will take the efforts of both of you to achieve this, but it takes only one partner to begin the process.

EXERCISE
How Apology Can Help Your Relationship

A. Sit in a quiet place where you won't be disturbed. Close your eyes and remember when you first fell in love with your partner. Remember the feeling of love and unconditional acceptance you once felt for him or her. Remember the hope you felt together. Let yourself bask in these feelings for a while. Allow these feelings to remind you of the love and mutual acceptance that are possible.

If these memories bring pain, let the tears flow. If they bring anger, write the angry feelings down on paper until they are out of your system, and then try to return to the memory of the love feelings.

B. Now with pen and pad in hand, remember all the things you loved, admired, and respected about your partner when you first fell in love. Write these qualities and characteristics down on paper.

If your hurt and anger make it difficult to remember these good qualities, spend some time writing about these feelings so that you can clear the path for the memories of the good qualities.

This exercise will set the stage for the real work—that of giving, receiving, and asking for one another's apologies.

1. Once again, go back in your mind to the beginning of the relationship. Imagine you have a remote control in your hand. Press the forward button on your imaginary remote control and watch as your life together slowly unfolds.

2. Try to remember the first time your partner hurt your feelings in a significant way, for example, the first time he criticized you, the first time she disappointed you by not keeping her word, or the first time he lied to you. For some people, these firsts have long been forgotten. Instead, they remember actual events—the time they got into an argument and he left her at the party all alone, the time she locked him out of the house and he had to sleep in the car, or the time he flirted openly with his best friend's date.

3. Write down these first memories.

4. Now press the forward button once again (slow forward as opposed to fast forward) and continue to watch the movie of your life together. Remember another event or series of events that hurt your feelings: the way he tends to ignore you when his mother visits, the way she got so caught up with the new baby that she didn't even seem to know you existed, the way he always turns over and falls asleep after sex, or the way she openly flirts with other men.

5. Write down these events and these hurts as they come to mind.

6. Continue slow forwarding your life together and writing down the hurts until you reach the present.

7. Take a look at all you've written down. You'll notice that some of your hurts may seem to pale in comparison to others. And you'll no doubt notice that even though you still remember some hurts, the feelings attached to these events aren't as strong as those attached to other events.

8. Circle those hurts or events that still zing you—the ones that still manage to upset you, hurt your feelings, or make you angry.

9. Now think about which of these hurts or events your partner apologized for, either at the time or later. It may be that he or she hasn't apologized to you for any of the items you circled—that's at least part of the reason why they still hurt so much.

10. Decide which of these items you would like to now ask your partner for an apology for. Even if he or she has already apologized, it is likely that either the apology felt insincere, it was forced out of him or her, or he or she continued the same behavior. (The one exception is if you've already received several apologies but none have seemed to do you any good. If this is the case, asking for another apology for the same offense isn't likely to work. Instead, you need to look at why you are holding onto your anger, resentment, or hurt. Refer to Chapter 6 for more help.)

Planning Your Apology Strategy

Ideally, your partner has already completed the above exercise. If this is not the case, encourage her or him to do so by sharing a little about your experience with the exercise.

It is important that you sit down together with your partner and make a plan for how you are going to proceed at this point. Here are some suggestions:

- Go over all your apology requests in one marathon session. Plan a day of it, or better yet, go away for a weekend trip together and devote your time and focus to apologizing to one another.

- Spend one evening a week for several weeks doing your apology work. It is usually best to divide the time somewhat equally, giving each partner a chance to process part of his or her list each time instead of letting one person complete his or her list before the other person begins his or hers. In this way, one person doesn't end up feeling like the bad guy.

- If one person has a long list and the other only a short one, the person with the longer list may want to shorten his or her list by combining items that are similar. For example, instead of listing 10 times when your partner disappointed you by arriving late, list the behavior as one item or list only the most significant times he arrived late (for your anniversary party, when you invited your best friend to dinner). You don't want to overwhelm your partner with a long list, since the point is not to make him or her feel like a horrible person or to dredge up each and every mistake but to elicit apologies that will help heal the relationship.

- If one of you refuses to make an apology request list, the other can still proceed. Tell your partner that after completing the above exercise you would like to ask for some apologies if he or she is willing to hear them.

How to Ask for Your Apologies

When you ask for an apology, you might say, "I'm still hurt about ___ and I need an apology from you." Remember to share your hurt feelings as opposed to attacking.

As much as possible, make direct statements and take responsibility for your feelings. For example:

> Do you remember when you were late for our anniversary party? Well, I'm still hurt about it. I know you apologized at the time, but I think you did it just to appease me. The point is, you were late because you had to work, and I think you feel that work should always come first—that you have a right to be late if you need to be at work. I realize I've been building up a lot of resentment about that for a long time without saying anything. But I want you to know that I want our marriage to come first to you and it hasn't seemed to for a long time. I guess I want an apology about that and I want to hear from you that you're going to make our marriage a priority.

How to Respond

Allow the other person to finish before saying anything. Then, if you feel that an apology is in order, do so. If you do not feel like apologizing, you can say so and explain why. Above all, don't allow yourselves to become involved in an argument. If someone doesn't feel like apologizing, let it go for the time being and move on to the next item. If, however, it becomes evident that one or both of you is unwilling to apologize for anything, end the exercise.

The important thing is that you are both committed to the process and that each of you has the intention of improving your relationship, letting go of your past anger, and repairing the harm of previous hurts. If one or both of you is not committed to this process, you may need to seek professional therapy or mediation to resolve your past issues. The following section may also help.

Starting Over with Apology

For years I have noticed that when couples enter therapy together it is often because one or both have unresolved anger toward each other. This was the case with Melanie and Jack, who were on the verge of divorce.

There was so much hostility between these two that it was palpable. Even though they each had a laundry list of complaints about everything from how they were treated to their sex life, it was difficult to ascertain exactly why they were each so intensely angry. It seemed as if all they did was find fault with each other, and they seemed to be so used to each other's putdowns that they could say the most horrible things and seemingly not hurt each other. They were in a constant "War of the Roses," with each one bent on outdoing the other.

When I gave them feedback to this effect and asked them why they stayed together when there was clearly so much animosity between them, they both stressed that they didn't want a divorce. I agreed to work with them to help save the marriage but didn't feel too optimistic. By the end of the second session, I suspected that something had started all their bickering and fault finding, that one or both had hurt the other terribly and from that time forward the battle was on, with each trying to one-up the other to see who could be the most cruel. When I voiced this suspicion, they both turned uncharacteristically quiet. "So, what started all this?" I asked, feeling I'd hit paydirt.

"It all started when he began flirting with everything in a skirt," Melanie said bitterly.

"Well, you sure paid me back, didn't you—in spades," countered Jack.

"I was just teaching you a lesson. Two can play at this game, you know," countered Melanie.

Before they got on a roll, I stopped them. "So what are you saying, Melanie? That Jack hurt you when he flirted and so you started flirting too?"

"Oh, she did more than that," Jack snorted. "She didn't get the reaction she was looking for by flirting, so she went out and had an affair!"

"Is that true, Melanie?"

Again, Melanie was uncommonly quiet. "Yeah, but I did it just to make him see how much his flirting hurt me."

"Flirting's one thing—an affair is something else entirely," said Jack.

"So you had an affair to teach him a lesson. Did you tell him about it? Did you continue the affair?" I asked.

"I only slept with the guy the one time—just to make a point. Yeah, I let Jack know. I was trying to get his attention and nothing else was working."

"And what happened after that?" I asked.

"Well, it stopped Jack from flirting, that's for sure. And we've been battling ever since," explained Melanie.

"So is that what all the fighting is about? The flirting and the affair?" I asked.

"Now that you put it that way, I guess so," said Jack. Melanie nodded in agreement. It might have been the first thing they'd agreed upon in years.

"So you never got over her affair?" I asked Jack. He looked down at his feet and said that no, he hadn't.

"And did you ever get over the fact that Jack had flirted with other women?" I asked Melanie.

"No, I never did. He said it was harmless and that he was just being a man, but it really hurt me. We were so much in love. He was everything to me and I couldn't stand it that I wasn't everything to him."

I asked Jack and Melanie if they were willing to try something and they agreed. As you read the description of what happened with Melanie and Jack, I suggest you imagine yourself doing the same exercise.

Face One Another with Honesty

I had Jack and Melanie sit in two chairs facing one another. "Melanie, I'd like you to tell Jack what you just told me, and I'd like you to look him directly in the eyes when you do," I instructed.

Reluctantly, Melanie repeated what she'd just said, looking into

Jack's eyes as she spoke. Even after all these years, tears started streaming down her face.

"Jack, can you see how much your flirting hurt Melanie?" I asked.

Jack nodded his head and was quiet for a moment. Then he asked Melanie, "But I stopped, didn't I?"

Melanie looked at Jack and said, "Yeah, you stopped, only because you were afraid I'd have another affair."

"Did you ever apologize to Melanie for hurting her?" I asked Jack.

"No, she got me back by having the affair. We were even."

"Evidently not," I said. "The battle's been raging for years."

"Well, I want it to stop," Jack said.

"Then you each need to tell the other how much you were hurt and apologize to one another."

In turn, each told the other how they had been hurt. Melanie explained to Jack how his flirting had made her doubt her attractiveness and how this had affected their sexual relationship. After he began flirting with other women, she said she never felt as spontaneous in the bedroom as she had before. She ended by saying, "When we first got married, I felt like the most beautiful woman in the world because you loved me. But when you started looking at other women, it broke my heart. I didn't feel beautiful anymore. I felt ugly." Tears streamed down her cheeks as she once again felt the pain.

And there were tears in Jack's eyes as well. "I never knew it hurt you so much. I didn't understand. I never wanted to hurt you. I thought you were just being silly. After all, all guys flirt. It was a macho thing to do in those days. I'm so sorry. I love you. I always have. You are the most beautiful woman in the world to me."

With that, Melanie reached out to Jack and pulled him toward her. They held one another and cried together quietly for a moment before they composed themselves and sat back in their respective chairs.

"I'd like you to ask Melanie if she would please forgive you for flirting with other women."

"Please forgive me. I didn't understand how much it hurt you."

Melanie looked Jack in the eyes and said, "I forgive you, Jack."

"Now it's your turn, Jack. I'd like you to tell Melanie how it felt for her to sleep with another man—even if it was just to teach you a lesson."

Jack was more hesitant. His face turned bright red and he looked embarrassed. "You taught me a lesson, but it was a painful one," he started out. "I can't even tell you how much it hurt."

He was quiet for at least a full minute. He twisted his hands in his lap. Finally, he almost whispered, "I've never been able to get the picture of you being in bed with that guy out of my mind. I see it all the time." With that he broke down in shuddering sobs.

In seconds Melanie was holding him. "Oh my God, oh my God," she said over and over. "I'm so sorry. I'm so sorry."

I remained quiet for several minutes, just letting them comfort one another. Although it may have seemed anticlimactic, there was one more piece of business to attend to.

"Melanie. I'd like you to ask Jack to forgive you for having the affair."

She did. "Will you forgive me, Jack? I know I did a horrible thing. I had no right to hurt you in that way. I wanted you to hurt like you'd hurt me, but I never realized it would hurt you this much. Please forgive me."

Through more deep sobs, Jack murmured, "I forgive you."

It had only taken two apologies to wipe out years and years of pain.

I saw Jack and Melanie for two more follow-up sessions to make sure there was no more residual anger and to teach some communication skills. There were a few more apologies to make for the hurts over the years, but having received the big apologies, they both were more than willing to forgive each other for the other hurts. I received a card from them 6 months later announcing that they were reaffirming their wedding vows.

Resolving Conflicts with Apology

Aside from disagreements concerning child rearing and major life decisions such as whether to buy a house or whether to have a child, most conflicts between couples have to do with one or both people feeling hurt by something their partner said, did, or did not do. For this reason, apology can help resolve most disputes between couples. Instead of constantly arguing over who did what, try really listening to your partner's side of the story and apologizing for your part in the problem. If both partners followed this simple plan, most disputes would be solved quickly, with both parties feeling heard and respected.

The problem is that most partners are so busy defending themselves or their position that they don't really hear their partner when he or she tries to express his or her feelings. And most partners are so caught up in feeling hurt and misunderstood that they can't apologize for their part in the conflict.

There existed a time when each person's word was respected, when people would listen to one another openly and carefully. But today most people are raised with the feeling that we are never really heard. As children, our words were experienced as a nuisance to adults. Today we are all so hungry to be heard that we cut one another off in an attempt to get our words out. Instead of listening openly without judgment, we are quick to question and contradict. Instead of recognizing that, above all else, our partner needs to be heard and have his or her feelings acknowledged, we defend and argue and stay focused on our own feelings.

We all want to be heard. We all want to be accepted. And ultimately we all want to be loved. Remembering this can help you to become more open-hearted when you talk to your partner. Being open-hearted means listening from the heart and speaking from the heart.

Listening from the Heart

When we listen from the heart, we listen openly and without judgment to what our partner is saying. We recognize that each person has a right to his or her own truth, opinions, and beliefs, and we do not try to impose our truths, opinions, or beliefs onto others. Listening from the heart asks us to find what Garfield, Spring, and Cahill, the authors of *Wisdom Circles*, call "the centerpoint of pure receiving," where we relax our assumptions and opinions to make room for new ideas, and where we can "show a greater degree of loving kindness."

The phrase "listening from the heart" also refers to the fact that partners are encouraged to listen with empathy and compassion. You attempt to experience as much as you can of the emotional life of the person speaking. Through your body posture, direct eye contact, attentiveness, and respectful silence, you can convey to your partner that you are listening empathetically—seeing through his or her eyes. You are willing to share in your partner's hopes and joys, to feel his or her fears and sorrows.

As you grow in your capacity to listen and empathize, you will find you are able to hear the deeper meanings of what is being said. You'll be able to understand the more subtle levels of communication that you may have previously missed.

Most importantly, you'll learn to appreciate the commonalities between you and your partner, and in turn grow to feel less separate from one another. By listening from your heart, you can expand your capacity for unconditional love. You can listen past those assumptions and expectations that prevented you from truly understanding one another.

Speaking from the Heart

When we speak from the heart, we say what is most true for us without censoring ourselves or trying to impress our partner. Speaking from the heart means we don't rehearse what we are going to say, but instead allow what is in our hearts and souls to come forth. As you increase your capacity to speak from the heart, you will become more and more aware of unconscious aspects of yourself and begin to hear even deeper, more meaningful words to say.

The following exercises will encourage you to practice listening and speaking from the heart and to use apology to resolve conflicts.

EXERCISE

Resolve Conflicts Through Open-Hearted Sharing

A. Without interrupting, take turns listening to the other person's perspective about what happened or what the problem is.

B. Now take turns apologizing to one another for your part in the disagreement or problem.

C. Focus on and discuss what you can learn from the experience as opposed to rehashing who did what. This may include agreeing to not repeat a particular scenario or thinking of ways to avoid similar conflicts.

EXERCISE
Put Yourself in Your Partner's Place

A. Make a list of the biggest complaints your partner has about you.

B. In the interest of saving your relationship or making it better, honestly assess each item, asking yourself if there is any truth to each complaint.

C. Put yourself in your partner's place and imagine what it would be like to have a partner who acts as you do.

CHAPTER 14

Teach Your
Children Well

*If there is anything we wish to change in the child, we should
first examine it and see whether it is not something that could
better be changed in ourselves.*

CARL JUNG

I n this chapter I discuss four aspects of apology as it relates to raising children: the importance of parents being positive role models to their children; the importance of parents teaching their
children to apologize; the importance of parents apologizing to
their children when they are impatient, inattentive, short-tempered,
or when they expect too much; and the importance of teaching children to ask for apologies instead of letting things build up.

Why model and teach apology? Children who learn apology and
have it modeled for them are far more likely to get along with others, to respect the rights and needs of others, and to develop a sense
of empathy and compassion for others.

When you encourage children to apologize, you teach them to
be responsible for their behavior. You encourage them to pay attention to their behavior and the effect it has on others and to put
themselves in the other person's place.

Children who can freely apologize tend to be less critical of
themselves when they make a mistake and to be less defensive when
others call them on their mistakes or inappropriate behavior.

They've learned that there is no loss of dignity in apologizing and that others actually tend to respect them more for doing so.

Parents as Role Models for Apology

Recent studies have confirmed what we all intuitively know: Parents have a more profound effect on their children's emotional and social development than any other influence—more than school, more than their peers. This is abundantly clear when you observe the role parents play in their children's ability to apologize. Children who hear their parents admit when they are wrong, apologize to one another, and forgive one another are far more likely to take on the same behavior than those who continually observe their parents blaming one another, holding grudges, or refusing to apologize or admit when they are wrong. The same holds true of children whose parents hold grudges or refuse to apologize to others outside the home. If you are a parent, ask yourself the following questions:

1. Do you tend to apologize to others when you make a mistake?

2. Do you apologize to your partner when you hurt, anger, or otherwise upset him or her?

3. Do you apologize to your partner in front of your children?

4. What lessons do you think your children are receiving concerning apology by watching how you and your partner relate to one another, or by observing your behavior with other people?

5. Do you apologize to your children when you hurt their feelings, neglect them, are overly critical, or expect too much of them?

Make no mistake about it—your children are constantly observing you, looking for clues about life, learning lessons about how they should treat other people. Observe your children as they play with others and you will see and hear your own behavior reflected back to you. If you have very young children, listen to how they play by themselves. As your young daughter plays with her dolls, she likely gives them each a voice. Listen to the dialogues between dolls for cues as to what she hears from you (and your partner, if you have one). Do her dolls argue and fight a lot with each other? Do you ever hear one of her dolls say "I'm sorry" to the other, or do you just hear her dolls blaming one another?

Recently, one of my clients, Nita, told me how she decided she needed to teach her stepdaughter about apology. The girl was very volatile, constantly blaming others for her own behavior and never apologizing when she was wrong.

Nita knew that Janey had grown up in a household where everyone was always fighting with each other and blaming each other. Nita's husband and his ex-wife had constantly argued, and now that Janey was reaching adolescence she had begun to argue with her father, who she thought was too strict with her.

One day the school called to report that Janey had cut class. As soon as she got into Nita's car after school, Janey began talking to Nita about how she knew she was going to get into trouble when her father came home. Nita thought that this was a great time to bring up the subject of apology. She advised Janey that instead of defending herself and arguing with her father, if she admitted she was wrong and apologized to him, he'd probably become a lot less angry with her.

When Janey's father got home, he sarcastically asked Janey how her day went (he'd already been informed about the cut class). Nita could see Janey's face harden in reaction. To defuse the situation, Nita said, "Janey was just telling me something very interesting. What were you saying, Janey?" Janey took the cue and meekly apologized for cutting class. Instead of getting enraged as was his usual pattern, her father quietly mentioned that they'd talk about it after dinner.

Later, he told Janey she was grounded for a week. Immediately, Janey began to rage at her father, and in reaction, he added a week. This really made Janey fly off the handle. She started yelling at her father that he was unfair, that he was a dictator and a horrible father.

To calm Janey down, Nita took her aside and once again explained that she needed to show her father that she was truly sorry. She explained that in essence his purpose in grounding her was to teach her a lesson. If she showed him she was truly sorry and that she had learned her lesson, he might lift the restriction. She stressed to her, however, that she needed to be sincere, not just be putting on an act.

The next Saturday, Janey was very helpful to her father. They worked in the yard all day together and later in the afternoon she went up to him, put her arms around him, and told him she really was sorry for yelling at him and that she deserved the restriction for cutting class. She also promised never to cut class again. As predicted, he lifted the restriction.

Janey came bounding into the house to tell Nita what had happened. While Nita told Janey she was happy for her, she once again stressed that we shouldn't apologize in order to manipulate others and get what we want out of them but because it feels better to apologize when we're wrong than to argue or blame others.

She asked Janey if she felt better after she'd apologized, first for cutting class and then for yelling at her father. Janey admitted that she felt better. The next thing Nita was going to work on was encouraging her husband to begin apologizing to his daughter.

The Benefits of Giving Apologies to Your Children

Parents are often reluctant to apologize to their children, even when they know they are wrong. They assume that apologizing will weaken their position or cause their children to lose respect for them. Some parents even believe that because they are the parents, they don't owe their children an apology.

But instead of weakening your position or damaging the image your children have of you, apologizing when your behavior or attitude toward them has been inappropriate, disrespectful, or too harsh will actually help your children gain more respect for you. We all sense that it takes a lot of courage to admit when we are wrong. Even children know this. By apologizing to your children when you are wrong, you become courageous in their eyes.

Apologizing to your children also tends to humanize you in their eyes. Instead of always seeing you as an authority figure, someone to fear or someone they can't hope to become, apologizing helps your children see you as another human being who, no matter how powerful or how accomplished, can also be vulnerable and can also make mistakes. This makes their own mistakes seem a little less egregious. Ironically, apologizing to your children doesn't cause them to feel that they have more permission to usurp your authority. Instead it causes them to identify more strongly with you and other authority figures.

By apologizing to your children, you show them that it is possible to admit you are wrong and still maintain your dignity. This will in turn encourage them to apologize when they are wrong.

One of the people who completed my questionnaire related this story: Her two children, Josh, age 7, and Heather, age 5, were playing in the backyard. After a few minutes, Heather came running into the house with tears streaming down her face. "Josh yelled at me and called me names," she cried.

Josh, who was close behind, said, "Well, you were acting like an idiot!" The woman comforted Heather and then turned to Josh. "Josh, I want you to tell Heather you're sorry for yelling at her. If you don't like something Heather's doing, all you have to do is tell her. There's no need for yelling or name-calling. I want you to apologize to her."

Josh looked up at her and said, "Well, you never apologize when you yell at me."

The woman sat dumbstruck. Her son was right. She did yell at her kids (even though she was trying not to) and she didn't apologize to them. She took Josh and Heather by the hands and told them, "You're right, Josh. I do yell and I don't apologize. I want you both to know that I am sorry I yell at you. I know it must hurt your feelings and I'm trying to stop. I'm going to try to do better."

Josh responded, "That's okay, Mom. We all make mistakes." Then he turned to Heather and said, "I'm sorry I yelled at you, Heather. You're not an idiot. You're just a little kid."

Overwhelmed with emotion, Heather gave her mother a big hug and said, "I love you, Mom." Then she turned to Josh and said, "I love you too, Josh, even though you are mean to me sometimes."

This example illustrates everything I've been telling you about children and apology. Children learn from their parents' behavior, so it's not enough just to teach your children to say they are sorry. You have to model it as well. And Josh and Heather didn't lose respect for their mother because she apologized—they gained respect for her.

Apologizing to your children shows them that you respect them, which will in turn help them to gain more respect for both you and themselves. My client, Marcie, apologized to her daughter, Stephanie (age 14), for not being a better mother when Stephanie was younger:

I wanted her to know that I knew I hadn't done a very good job of raising her. I wanted to get it all out in the open instead of having it be in the air but remain unspoken. I'm a good mother now and I know she appreciates it, but I also know it doesn't really make up for the way I was in the past.

When I apologized for neglecting her and for shipping her off to her father's just because I was stressed out, she started to cry. I hugged her and let her cry for a while, and then she dried her eyes and said, "I've been waiting for that apology for a long time, Mom. I needed to hear those words. I needed you to tell me you knew how hard it was for me. I knew you were sorry and I forgave you already, but now I respect you so much more for saying the words."

By apologizing to your children, you validate their feelings and perceptions. You let them know that they have a right to feel hurt or to be angry with you when you are insensitive.

It is very difficult for children to allow themselves to feel anger toward their parents, especially very young children, because they are so dependent on their parents for their physical as well as emotional well-being. Getting angry at a parent can feel very threatening. After all, from a child's perspective, when someone knows you are angry with her, she can get angry back and she can go away from you.

Even older children tend to deny (consciously and unconsciously) when they are angry toward a parent. Most children love their parents very much and don't want to hurt their parents' feelings. And anger separates people. When we are angry with someone, we feel our separateness from him or her—a state that most children don't want to feel.

Tyler, age 14, is a case in point. For several years he had been angry with his mother for marrying a man who was emotionally and physically abusive to her and for staying with this man. But Tyler's anger remained hidden from his consciousness. After all, he loved his mother. And he rationalized that it wasn't her fault. She wasn't the bad person; his stepfather was. She couldn't help it that she'd married an abusive man. He didn't understand why she didn't leave him, but he figured it was because she loved him so much.

It wasn't until several years later, after his mother had finally left his stepfather, that Tyler was able to express his anger toward his mother. As far as Tyler's mother, Marian, was concerned, everything was going really well for her and Tyler. She was much happier since she'd gotten her divorce, and she and Tyler had become closer than ever. But suddenly Tyler began acting out. He stole some money from her purse and he began sneaking out of the house at night.

Marian had been seeing me for counseling to help her overcome the effects of her abusive marriage. When she told me about Tyler's new behavior, I asked her if she'd ever talked with Tyler about her abusive marriage. She said that they often talked about how much happier they were now that they were away from her exhusband, but that was the extent of it.

I encouraged her to talk to Tyler, to ask him how he felt about the fact that she'd married such a man and had stayed with him even after he'd begun abusing her. I explained to her that Tyler was likely angry with her but unable to express his anger directly; thus, the stealing and sneaking out of the house.

She agreed it was important to have a talk with Tyler, but when I saw her the next time she reported that the conversation hadn't gone very well. He admitted to being angry with his stepfather, but when she asked him if he was angry with her, he changed the subject and just shrugged. As I had advised her to do, she did tell him that he had a right to be angry with her and asked if he'd like to talk to me. He showed some interest, so Marian asked me to see him for a session.

As he had with his mother, Tyler expressed a great deal of anger toward his stepfather. Realizing that it was therapeutic to let him express his anger, I encouraged him to tell me why he was angry with his stepfather and what he'd like to do to him. He reported that it felt good to let his anger out in this way—that his mother always told him he shouldn't think revengeful thoughts, so he'd always cut off his anger in the past.

Before the session was over, I wanted to address the subject of his anger toward his mother. I explained to Tyler that it was perfectly normal for him to be angry with his mother for staying in such an abusive relationship. Then I asked him if he was, in fact, angry with her. At first he had a difficult time coming out with it, but eventually he admitted that he was angry with her.

We spent the rest of the session talking about how he felt about the fact that she'd stayed with an abusive man (he felt angry, hurt, and disappointed) and what effect this had on him (it made him feel helpless, made him afraid of his own anger, and caused him to fear that he too might end up being abusive).

Since Marian was my client, it wasn't appropriate for me to continue to see Tyler. At our next session I recommended she get him into a group therapy situation with other children who had witnessed abuse. I also asked her if she'd ever apologized to Tyler for putting him in this position, and she said that she hadn't. I explained that it was very important for her to apologize. First, it would validate Tyler's perceptions that she'd been wrong to stay with an abusive man and would reinforce that he had good reason to be angry with her. Second, it would show him that she recognized that she had, in fact, damaged him by keeping him in an abusive situation. Finally, it would give him a feeling of power—something he needed to experience since he felt powerless with his stepfather and powerless to help his mother. By apologizing to Tyler, she would essentially give him the power to forgive her or not.

In Marian's case, her son already saw her as weak and was angry at her for this weakness. She had nothing to lose by apologizing and everything to gain—her son's understanding and compassion being the most valuable rewards. After she apologized to Tyler, she reported feeling a huge wave of relief pass over her. She hadn't realized it, but she had been carrying around a tremendous amount of guilt and shame for staying in an abusive relationship and exposing her son to an abusive man. Her apology helped relieve her of that guilt and shame. Her son's forgiveness relieved it even more.

Limiting Apologies

You will need to be careful not to go to extremes with apologizing. Do not continually apologize for all your shortcomings or for every little mistake you make with your children, or you risk spoiling them or becoming weak in their eyes. Start by apologizing for the significant mistakes you made in the past and then continue to apologize when you are neglectful or too harsh. Remember that an apology made to a child is intended to help heal the harm you've caused, to show respect, and to model apology. Apology should not be used to ingratiate yourself to your child, to placate an angry child, or as an excuse to continue the same behavior.

Actions truly do speak louder than words. If you apologize to your children for behavior that you continue to exhibit, soon your apologies will seem empty and meaningless. Instead of modeling the value of apology, you will actually turn your children against apologizing, since it will become a hypocritical act in their eyes. An apology only has power when it is followed by a concerted effort to not repeat the offense. Although no one is perfect or should aim for perfection, your children should be able to recognize your efforts to change behavior that has caused them pain or unhappiness in the past.

How to Receive an Apology from Your Children

If you are going to teach your children the importance of apology, you will need to be able to receive and accept apologies from them in such a way that encourages them to apologize to you. For example, when your children apologize, don't:

- Continue to berate them for the behavior they are apologizing for
- Bring up other offenses they have committed
- Tell them you know they are not really sorry
- Tell them that saying they're sorry isn't good enough

The Benefits of Asking Your Children for an Apology

Even though we are often not aware of it, little irritants and resentments can build up to the point where we begin to close our hearts to the ones we love. It goes something like this: You made a special effort to leave work early so that you could come home and make a nice dinner for your family. You stop at the store and buy all your son's favorites and then rush home to begin the preparations. Even though you're tired, you don't take any shortcuts. When your son comes home with two of his friends, he looks surprised and disappointed that you are already home. You can understand this, since he probably wanted his privacy, so you make a point of assuring them that they can go into the den and won't be disturbed. You make his friends feel welcome and ask them if they'd like a drink and a snack. When they say yes, you stop what you are doing to make them some sandwiches. Your son not only doesn't thank you for making the snack but complains about the kind of sandwiches you made. Determined to not let anything spoil your special night, you talk yourself out of being hurt by reminding yourself that your son is only 15.

You finish your preparations and put your special dinner in the oven. As it gets close to the time for your husband to arrive home, you politely ask your son to turn down the stereo, which has been blaring for over 2 hours. Your son shoots you a look that could kill, turns off the stereo, and storms out of the house yelling over his shoulder, "Thanks a lot for ruining my afternoon, Mom!" Hurt and angry, you watch as his two friends sheepishly follow him through the back door. You're certain he won't be home for dinner.

That evening you and your husband have a lovely dinner together and he thanks you profusely for your efforts. You love your husband very much and enjoy doing things for him, but in the back of your mind you can't let go of your anger toward your son for being so rude and unappreciative, and you wish he'd been home to enjoy the dinner too, especially since it was his favorite meal.

By the next morning, your son has forgotten all about the previous afternoon and is his usual cheerful self. While you secretly hope for an apology, you know from experience that it won't be forthcoming, so you try to let it go. But the sad truth is you never really do. The next time you have the idea to make his favorite meal, you remember this last incident and think better of it. The next time his friends come over, you are a little less cordial and less tolerant of their loud music.

Instead of harboring your hurt and anger, it would have been far better for you to take your son aside the next day and tell him how hurt and angry you were at his behavior and that you feel he owed you an apology. It would also let him know that his behavior was unacceptable and that you weren't willing to put up with it in the future.

Unfortunately, we become so full of anger and resentment due to our daily experiences of being hurt, unappreciated, neglected, or ignored that our loving feelings for our partner or our children become buried under the hotbed of our seething anger. We become less generous and caring and more impatient and intolerant.

The following suggested activities—apology night and the apology box—provide a way for everyone in the family to ask for the apologies they need in a safe, nonthreatening format.

Apology Strategies for the Entire Family

In this section I present two important strategies specifically designed to teach children to apologize, to ask for apologies, and to facilitate the healing of family relationships through apology: *apology night* and *apology boxes*. Both strategies have the following benefits:

- They help children learn right from wrong.
- They help children develop empathy.
- They teach responsibility.
- They teach children that their behavior has an effect on others and that there are consequences for their actions.
- They keep the lines of communication open between parents and their children.
- They help create and maintain connectedness with family members.
- They help all family members, especially children, release anger and resentment in a constructive way.
- They help resolve guilt and shame.
- They help children feel they are listened to.

Apology Night

Each member of the family should be able to participate in this activity, no matter what their age. Even though it probably isn't wise or productive to have children under the age of 6 (the age when most children have developed a social conscience) participate by apologizing, younger children can benefit from receiving apologies and can learn the importance of apologizing by listening to other family members apologize to one another. If a younger child wishes to apologize to another family member, he or she can be allowed to do so, but it shouldn't be expected. (If a younger child is too disruptive, you may wish to wait until he or she is in bed.) Here are some suggested guidelines:

- Set aside one evening a week (perhaps a night when you can all have dinner together) to sit down together for an hour. Make it clear to everyone that this is not a night to schedule outings with friends and try not to make it when someone's favorite TV program will be coming on right after dinner. Unplug the phone, turn off the TV, and let friends and relatives know that this is not a night when they are welcome to drop by.

- If you already have a family night, simply add apology night to your existing plans. Feel free to add other elements you feel are important, such as also setting aside a time for gratitude or a time to share how much you appreciate one another.

- Allow a different family member to be the spokesperson for the group each week. This person will start and end the meeting and facilitate the group interaction throughout.

- Begin each meeting by having someone state your group intention out loud. Generally speaking, your intention should be to bring the family closer together by airing complaints and apologizing to one another for slights and mistakes. Variations of this intention might be:

  "We are a family and we love each other. The purpose of our meeting together is to mend the hurt feelings that get in the way of us feeling and acknowledging our love and support for one another."

  "We all say and do things that hurt other family members. Tonight we meet to apologize for the hurt we may have caused other family members, however unintentional."

- Some begin their apology night by holding hands and sitting quietly together for a few moments. You may also wish to designate the time and space as special or sacred by lighting a candle or incense, by reading a poem or quote out loud, by singing a song together, or by saying a prayer. The spokesperson may wish to be in charge of deciding how the group will start.

Ready, Set, Begin

The following directions will guide you in conducting family apology night:

1. Have paper and pens ready for each family member. The spokesperson will ask each person to make two lists:

- A list of all the things you've done (or left undone) to others in the family that you wish to apologize for
- A list of all the things you feel others in the family have done to you that you feel warrant an apology

Allot approximately 10 minutes for each person to make his or her list.

2. Each family member will begin by reading from his or her list those things he or she wishes to apologize for. The person may wish to apologize to the family as a whole for a certain behavior or attitude, or to each family member he or she has wronged. You can determine which order to take by either moving around the circle or by asking for volunteers.

3. When someone apologizes, the response from the other person (or persons) should be either:

- "I accept your apology," *or*
- "I appreciate your apology because what you did hurt my feelings (or made me angry)."

Just because someone apologizes doesn't mean the other person (or persons) will be ready to forgive. But by saying the second statement, you are at least acknowledging the apology, which is very important.

4. Don't take away the apology by minimizing or making excuses for what the other person did. Refrain from saying any of the following types of comments:

- "Oh, it wasn't any big deal."
- "You don't need to apologize."
- "I shouldn't be so sensitive."
- "I shouldn't have _____" (implying that you *caused* the other person's behavior).

5. Don't go into a diatribe about how much you were hurt or how much the other person's behavior bothered you. This is not the time or place to air angry feelings. If you aren't ready to forgive and you need to have a discussion with the other person, wait until you can be alone or make an appointment for a discussion at a later time.

6. Don't say you *don't* accept the other person's apology. You may need more time, but your intention should be to work toward forgiveness. If you aren't prepared to do so, you shouldn't take part in apology night.

7. After each person has had a chance to read their first list and to apologize, hold hands, take a deep breath, and look around the circle, making eye contact with each other, appreciating the support and love that you share.

8. Before ending, ask that everyone tear up the paper they used to write both their lists. Some families like to tear up the lists as a group and then toss them in the air as a ritual of their letting go. If some group members aren't prepared to let go, either because they did not receive an apology they felt they were owed or because they need more time to let the apology they received sink in, these members will keep their lists and not tear them up. This will be a visible reminder that more work needs to be done.

   Often, even though a family member didn't actually receive an individual apology for the specific offense he or she listed, a general apology may have been given to the entire family and this may feel sufficient. Or this person may have received an apology from the offending party about a similar behavior or attitude. In these situations, it is common for the family member to want to tear up his or her list.

9. If anyone still feels that he or she is owed an apology, this person has two options:

   - Give a note to the offending party stating why he feels he is owed an apology. The person then has the option to either personally apologize, wait for the next apology night, or make an appointment to discuss the issue privately.

   - Take the person aside and set up an appointment to discuss the reasons why he feels an apology is owed.

10. As time goes on, you may wish to add a second part to the process: allowing everyone in the family to read their second list and to state why they feel they are owed an apology if it has not been forthcoming. This gives family members the opportunity to actually air their feelings and allows the wrongdoer to hear how his or her behavior affected another family member. This

is not an invitation for a major discussion or argument, however. Instead, the person who is requesting an apology simply states why she feels she is owed one and how the other person's behavior affected her. The other person is to listen *in silence* without arguing or making excuses. When it is his turn, he is then allowed to say one of the following statements:

- "I am sorry I hurt you. It wasn't my intention."
- "You're right. I do owe you an apology. I'm sorry."
- "Thank you for telling me about this. I'll think about what you said."
- "I didn't realize you felt this way about it. Give me some time to think about it and I'll get back to you on it."

Under no circumstances should two family members be allowed to argue about what has been said. It is equally important for other family members to stay out of the process. There should be no taking sides. The only intervention that other members should make is to offer a reminder of the rules.

No one, especially children, should ever be made to feel that they are wrong for wanting an apology or for feeling hurt. Neither should anyone be allowed to try to talk family members out of their feelings, minimize their pain, or make fun of them.

Apology night is a democratic endeavor—each member of the family is to be treated equally. Children and teenagers have just as much right to be apologized to as adults, and they will respect their parents for being big enough to admit their mistakes. Parents should take off their parental hats and put them aside for the evening by refraining from correcting or lecturing their children or coaching them on how to say their apology. If a child needs to be reminded of the rules, the spokesperson should be the one to do so. It may help younger children to have the rules written out for them to refer to.

Children under 6 should not be expected to understand the concept of apology and therefore should not be expected to apologize for their behavior, no matter how egregious. Very young children aren't capable of regretting their actions. Making them apologize is really just encouraging them to be insincere.

Obviously parents may wish to save their more intimate apologies for a private apology session later the same night or at another designated time. Generally speaking, issues such as sexuality, infidelity, money, or differences in child rearing need to be dealt with privately, not in front of children, but everyday slights and mistakes such as being rude, impatient, inconsiderate, or short-tempered are fair game for apology night. Children need healthy role models for taking responsibility for their behavior and to learn positive methods of conflict resolution. An added benefit is that when children hear their parents acknowledging their own mistakes and shortcomings, they feel less inadequate themselves. Also, children will feel relieved to know that their parents can apologize to one another instead of holding grudges or arguing incessantly, and this will help them feel more secure about their parents' ability to stay married and keep the family intact.

The Apology Box

If the idea of an apology night doesn't suit your needs or personalities, I have yet another suggestion. Do you remember the Jewish students I mentioned earlier in the book who, during the Jewish Day of Atonement, placed little notes on the bulletin board asking the forgiveness of those they have hurt or offended during the year? Taking off on this idea, why not create such a tradition in your family? You can do so by putting up a bulletin board or leaving a box in a designated place. If you don't want others to read your apology, put it in a sealed envelope with the person's name on it.

You may wish to conduct this tradition at a time that will coincide with a special holiday, such as New Year's Day, when our minds naturally turn to such issues as forgiveness and making a new start. Better yet, don't wait for a holiday that comes only once a year to honor your tradition. Once a month will be far more conducive to clearing up past hurts and not letting them fester.

CHAPTER 15

Healing Your Business Relationships Through Respect and Compassion

I can't help thinking how much nicer the work and home environment would be if everybody learned to say they were sorry—and to move on.

DEBORAH TANNEN (*LADIES' HOME JOURNAL*, SEPTEMBER 1994)

⚛

Apology makes all business relationships run more smoothly. It fosters respect, compassion, and trust in business relationships, whereas the absence of apology often fosters anger, pettiness, and distrust.

Apologizing when you don't perform at your optimum level, when you don't perform at the level a customer or client expected, or because of an oversight or mistake on your part or on the part of someone else in the company can do more to boost your client or customer's opinion of you and/or the company you represent than almost anything else. The same holds true of the power of apology to affect the work environment. Apologizing to a co-worker, supervisee, or employee when you have been impatient, rude, or inconsiderate can do more to develop and maintain an effective, cooperative, and healthy work environment than almost any other action you can take.

In this chapter we discuss apology as it relates to business, as well as focus on how apologizing and asking for apologies teaches us how to be more compassionate in our business dealings.

Apology—The Ultimate Way of Showing Respect

Respect should be the most important aspect of our business relationships. Although we don't have to like the people with whom we work or do business, we need to respect them. Apologizing when we have made a mistake, committed an oversight, or offended someone is beyond a doubt one of the most significant ways of showing respect. By the same token, *not* apologizing when we have done any of these things is one of the most blatant ways of showing disrespect.

When we don't apologize to a client, business associate, co-worker, or employee who feels offended, we are in essence conveying the message that we don't care about their feelings. Apologizing when we have made a mistake or committed an oversight conveys a message of regret and concern on our part and an acknowledgment that the other person has a right to be upset.

Don't Blame the Client or Customer

Unfortunately, there is a subtle yet pervasive trend in American culture (as well as many other cultures) to blame the client or customer. Instead of "the customer is always right," we've devolved to an attitude of "the customer is a pain in the neck." Instead of immediately apologizing for a mistake or oversight, we make excuses, blame someone else, or even act insulted because the customer or client is complaining. We become defensive and even belligerent instead of going out of our way to make up for the mistake.

For those who are in customer service or who work with individual clients, think back to the last time a customer or client complained to you. Did you immediately apologize or did you become defensive? Did you admit the mistake or did you blame someone else? Were you gracious or did you act put out?

Unfortunately, many businesspeople don't even stop to think about the fact that they did, in fact, make a mistake. Therefore, they don't learn from their mistakes and don't improve their service. As customers continue to complain, they simply hide behind the attitude of defensiveness, indifference, and even hostility. The same problems exist in other working environments. Lawyers, doctors, and other health care professionals are notorious for pompously making those who dare question them feel like they are idiots or troublemakers.

Adding Insult to Injury

We've all had the experience of being wronged in a business situation only to have the other person deny it, ignore it, or even turn it around and blame us. This, as the expression goes, adds insult to injury. Not only is the other person unwilling to apologize and try to rectify the situation, but he or she has insulted and disrespected us by blaming us.

And we've all had the experience of complaining to a businessperson about some aspect of service only to have this person act as if we were being unreasonable. It's not an uncommon occurrence today to have store clerks actually roll their eyes or make a face when they receive a complaint.

Sometimes the insult is to our intelligence; other times the insult is to our word of honor. There is nothing more insulting than to be wronged and then be accused of lying about the situation. Sometimes the only way to restore a sense of personal honor may be to file a formal or legal complaint, thereby forcing the injuring party to face up to what he or she has done.

Passing the Buck

Another common practice in business environments today is that of passing the buck. This often occurs in business offices, corporations, and major institutions where more than one person is working on a project or where it takes several steps (and several different people and departments) to produce a product. When something goes wrong, it's easy to say that the other guy is responsible rather than to simply apologize. For example, if a deadline isn't met, it's far more common to say that your department didn't get its supplies in time than to apologize for the delay.

Solving Disputes Through Apology

Apology is beyond a doubt the single most effective method of resolving business disputes. Unfortunately, many people are too proud, too stubborn, or too insecure to admit when they are wrong. Add to this the fear of lawsuits that permeates our business environments and you can see why apology is often difficult.

It is often the insecure person who cannot admit when he or she is wrong—who has to vehemently defend himself or herself at all costs. A more secure person can admit he made a mistake or at least be open to the possibility, since being wrong is not a horrible thing to him and does not affect his self-esteem.

Some people believe that it is a matter of pride to never admit they have made a mistake. Others live by the belief that since no one can prove they are wrong, they will maintain their innocence at all costs. *(As long as I continue to deny it, I'll get away with it.)* But there is an arrogance in both these stances that comes through loud and clear and is insulting to the other person—so insulting that the other person may be willing to take legal action.

Think back to an incident when all you wanted from a business exchange or relationship was an apology in order for you to put the incident behind you. Remember how you felt when the apology was not forthcoming? Were you insulted? Were you so insulted that you pursued other measures?

A large percentage of lawsuits and formal complaints against businesses, employers, or co-workers would not be filed if a simple apology were given. In addition, because of the absence of an apology, many people have been fired, demoted, or passed over for promotions.

Advice to Employers, Supervisors, and Directors

While it can often feel as if you are constantly in the middle between the customer/client and your employees, or between one department and the other, the fact is that if you are the boss, the supervisor, or the director, the buck stops with you. An honorable employer or supervisor recognizes this and doesn't hide behind his or her employees or supervisees. If something goes wrong, he or she immediately apologizes to the customer or client and assures the customer that the problem will be solved. This person shows customers respect by acknowledging that they have been inconvenienced.

A customer or client who has been inconvenienced or disappointed in a product or outcome wants three things:

1. He or she wants an *apology*. An apology is an acknowledgment that the customer or client has been harmed, inconvenienced, or disappointed and is a statement of regret.

2. The customer or client wants to be *heard*. There is nothing more frustrating than receiving less than adequate service and then feeling like your righteous feelings of anger, frustration, or disappointment are being minimized or ignored.

3. He or she wants someone to *take responsibility* for the mistake or oversight, in addition to *assurance that the problem will be rectified*. You can't change what's been done, but you can assure the customer that the error will be remedied or that the same mistake will not happen again.

An employer or supervisor who blames someone else for the problem instead of providing the customer or client with these three aspects of apology will not be respected by the customer, his or her employees, or supervisees. He or she will be seen as weak and as a coward.

Neither does it look good for an employer or supervisor to constantly blame his or her customers or clients. It sets a precedent, encouraging employees and supervisees to do the same. This attitude will soon permeate the entire workplace, lowering morale and giving everyone an excuse to mess up. If no one respects or cares about the recipients of the product or service you are providing, then what is the point in striving for excellence or for providing the best service possible?

When an employer or supervisor shows respect toward the customer or client by immediately apologizing for delays, mistakes, or oversights, and by immediately assuring the client that the problem will be resolved one way or another, that employer or supervisor models a respect for the client or customer to all those who work for or with him or her. It's as simple as this: If you respect those with whom you are doing business, you are going to try harder. And if everyone is trying harder, customers and clients are going to be happier and your business is going to thrive, or you are going to advance up the ladder a lot faster.

Apologizing Even When
You've Done Nothing Wrong

While there can be few things harder than apologizing when you don't feel you've done anything wrong, in business there are times when you must do just that if you want to be respected and successful. If you have an upset client or customer, something must be done to remedy the situation. Usually this involves an apology of some kind on your part. This doesn't mean you have to take responsibility for something you didn't do, but you do need to provide the three aspects of effective apology: acknowledgment, regret, and an attempt to remedy the situation.

A friend of mine owns a small, independent bookstore in California, and she deals with the public every day. On most days it is fairly quiet, with only one or two customers in the store at a time, so she works the counter herself. Every once in a while, however, there will be a rush of customers for no apparent reason, and at times they all end up at the counter at one time. When this happens, most customers are understanding, but there is occasionally one who is in a big hurry and grows impatient. Although my friend doesn't feel she has done anything wrong—she certainly couldn't help it that the customers all decided to check out at the same time—she has found that it is very important to apologize to all her customers, whether they seem impatient or not:

> As soon as the customer reaches the head of the line, I say, "I'm terribly sorry that you had to wait." If a customer hasn't felt put out, they almost always say, "Oh, no problem." If they have grown impatient, it almost always quiets their anger and he or she ends up nodding or mumbling something about it being okay. Once in a while, someone will say something like, "You should hire another clerk," or "Tell the owner to hire another person," depending upon whether they think I'm the owner or not, but otherwise most don't say anything more.
>
> Depending on my mood and the mood of the customer, I sometimes explain that it isn't cost-effective for me to have someone else in the store, or that it happens so rarely that customers all line up like this that it doesn't make sense to hire

another person. I've noticed that when I've explained this to regular customers, they tend to be less impatient if it happens again.

The reason my friend's strategy works so well is that by apologizing right away for the inconvenience she does three things:

1. She acknowledges there was a problem and a reason for their impatience.
2. She shows customers respect by acknowledging that they shouldn't have to wait.
3. She expresses regret for the inconvenience.

In turn, the customers' anger is defused. Customers feel that the fact that they were inconvenienced has been *acknowledged* and so they don't really have to verbalize this themselves. And, most important, customers feel *respected*. Even though my friend doesn't offer a remedy to the situation, most customers continue to be fine with the way things are.

Dealing with an Unreasonable or Irate Customer or Client

In business we not only have to apologize when we haven't done anything wrong, but sometimes we have to apologize even when the customer or client is being completely unreasonable. I'll give you an example from my own experience.

Several years ago when I had a practice in the Los Angeles area, workmen began to tear up the street just in front of my offices. It was noisy and messy. My clients were used to parking on this street and now had to find parking spaces around the block. When the work first began, I apologized to my clients for the inconvenience, and most seemed fine with the situation. But one particular client was very upset and my apology didn't seem to appease her. Instead she seemed to blame me for the inconvenience and threatened to stop coming to me if I didn't do something about the situation.

Granted, it is my job to understand where people are coming from and to maintain a nondefensive stance, but even therapists can have a problem maintaining their cool when being attacked. The woman's voice had risen and she was becoming verbally abusive to me, yet I knew that I needed to defuse the situation by letting her know I was really hearing her. I did this by paraphrasing what she had already said: "I hear that the roadwork outside has made you very upset. You were running late and not finding a parking space made you even more late."

Paraphrasing what my client had said served two purposes: First, it let her know I had really heard what she had to say, that I was really listening to her. Second, it helped me to understand what the *real issue* was for her, to get to what psychotherapists call the "meta-message"—the message within the message. In this case, the meta-message was that my client very much needed to see me and she was afraid she was going to miss her appointment.

Realizing this, I said to her, "I understand that you really needed to see me today and that you were afraid you'd miss your appointment." As soon as the words were out of my mouth, she quieted down.

All that was left for me to do at this point was to reassure her and to try to remedy the situation. I explained to her that even if she was late, she wouldn't miss her appointment, that I considered this her hour and would wait the entire hour for her. Next, I suggested that she turn down another street next week, avoiding the roadwork entirely, and that she park on a particular street where I knew there was ample parking.

Even though I had personally done nothing wrong, it was still my obligation to apologize for the inconvenience my clients would incur due to the roadwork. And as a sign of respect and courtesy, I needed to acknowledge my client's feelings about the situation.

By *acknowledging* your customer or client's feelings, *apologizing* for the problem, and then *remedying* the situation, you will find that most problems can be easily and calmly solved. Both you and your customer or client will feel better.

Finally, by looking for the meta-message, you can diffuse even the most irate client's anger. Although most people aren't trained to look for or discover the meta-message, as psychotherapists are, it is not a difficult skill to learn if put your mind to it.

When a customer or client is upset, listen for the real reason for the problem. Start by looking for what he or she is *afraid* of. For example, he or she may be afraid of not being able to meet a dead-line, of not getting a product in time, or of not being compensated for the mistake.

If you think I am being ridiculous to suggest that you go to all this trouble to quiet an irate customer or client, think about the situation from another perspective. Haven't we all become unexplainably upset over a somewhat minor inconvenience? If the businessperson seemed indifferent or even rude to you, didn't your anger then escalate? Now think of a time when, instead of ignoring you or making you feel like an idiot, the businessperson really listened to you, apologized, and assured you that the problem would never happen again. Didn't this calm you down? Wasn't this a much better way of handling the situation?

How Apology Can Be Used to Improve Your Relationships with Co-workers and Employees

People who work together usually represent a mixture of personality types, communication styles, and political, racial, and religious backgrounds. On top of this, when people work together day in and day out, they often become impatient with one another or irritated with one another's behavior, similar to the situation that occurs in families.

It should not be surprising then to find that disputes and difficulties arise often in the work environment. It should also not be surprising to discover that most employees are unaware that some of their behavior is experienced as irritating, insensitive, or inconsiderate by their co-workers. Instead, most people tend to focus on the behavior of their co-workers when there is a problem.

To prove this point, let me share with you a common experience that occurs during the apology seminars I conduct for businesses. I ask participants to list their co-workers' behavior that is most irritating or upsetting to them and to explain why it is upsetting or hurtful. Then I have each person read his or her list out loud while sitting in a circle. Many are shocked when they hear other people describe behavior they themselves are guilty of and discover that their own behavior is as upsetting to others as the behaviors they listed.

While each employee is not expected to apologize individually to every person he or she may have irritated or hurt, I do have each person who feels like it apologize to the group for any behavior on his or her part that he or she feels may have been insensitive, inconsiderate, or irritating. Those who volunteer to do this report feeling somewhat embarrassed initially but feeling much better about themselves afterward. In follow-up evaluations they report feeling closer to their fellow workers and having a far less stressful work environment.

Although more and more businesses are conducting workshops such as my apology seminars, not everyone is fortunate enough to experience them. But this doesn't mean you can't receive the benefits of apology by making sure you apologize to your co-workers when you are impatient, irritable, rude, or inconsiderate. We all have bad days and no one can expect us to be perfect, but your co-workers deserve to be treated with respect and to receive an apology when your behavior is hurtful. By the same token, when a co-worker apologizes to you, be a big enough person to accept the apology instead of continuing to pout. Remember that it is highly possible that you have either done something to irritate or hurt this same co-worker or other co-workers.

Ask for an apology from a co-worker who has hurt or angered you instead of giving him or her the cold shoulder, complaining about him or her to other co-workers, or planning a way to get back at him or her.

Be Flexible

As we've been discussing, the act of apology can be profoundly beneficial in business settings. But we need to be flexible. As Deborah Tannen, author of *The Argument Culture*, warns, people have different conversational styles, contexts vary, and the same thing will not work well with every person. If we apologize to a business associate in order to be polite and considerate, and he or she shares this conversational trait, it can help to create a smooth relationship. But in cases where the other person doesn't share your conversational style, your ritual apologies can be taken literally and your real apologies may be misconstrued as weakness, particularly in a business setting. This is especially true for women, since women who constantly apologize to co-workers or business associates may begin to be seen as incompetent.

Although respect and courtesy will always pay off in any business setting, overapologizing or constantly taking the blame when you did nothing wrong will only cause your work colleagues and business associates to lose respect for you. People who wish to climb the corporate ladder need to make certain they don't negatively affect their image by excessive apologizing.

Through the respect and compassion that apology communicates and inspires, you can improve all your business relationships, whether they are important contacts you have with your customers or clients, or the day-in and day-out interactions you have with your co-workers or employees. You spend a great deal of your life at work. By making it a point to give, accept, and ask for apologies on a regular basis, you can make work a far more pleasant environment for you and everyone else.

CHAPTER 16

Conclusion: The Apology Movement

The practice of forgiveness is our most important contribution to the healing of the world.

MARIANNE WILLIAMSON

*T*he *Power of Apology* is not only a book to me but a cause. My deepest desire is that many of you will make large and small apologies an integral part of your daily life. By apologizing for your oversights, mistakes, and transgressions, you will give others the respect they deserve, reinforce your resolve to treat others with more kindness, and continue to increase your level of empathy and compassion.

By making amends for the offenses that have harmed others, you will cleanse yourself of esteem-robbing shame and guilt and give those you've offended one of the most beneficial gifts they will ever receive.

By teaching your children the importance of apology and by showing them how to make meaningful apologies, you will give them a head start in life. Teaching children to apologize also teaches them humility and the importance of taking responsibility for their actions. Children who understand the importance of apology tend to be more respectful, compassionate, and patient toward others.

By apologizing for your daily oversights, you show your partner and your children respect and caring, and model empathy and compassion to your children. By apologizing to your partner for past offenses, you will help him or her to heal old wounds that have been festering and robbing your relationship of trust and intimacy.

The Seeds of the Apology Movement

The seeds of the apology movement were planted by the teachings of most religions and by 12-step programs many years ago. In Japan, apologies are part of the cultural fabric. But it has only been in the past several years that the potential for a full-fledged movement has begun to emerge as evidenced by the following:

1. It has become increasingly common for governments and churches to reconsider their past and to apologize for past misdeeds in order to start fresh in the 21st century. All over the world there seems to be a deep and abiding interest in apologizing for the wrongs committed by governments, religious organizations, and sometimes entire nations.

2. An important aspect of the Million Man March was apologizing and making restitution to women and children for not protecting and providing for them.

3. In south-central Los Angeles, the Grace Church began what is now referred to as the "Sister, I'm Sorry Movement," where male members of the church apologize for the wrongs such as abandonment, rape, and sexual abuse that other men have done to female members of the church. This process has now spread to other churches.

4. There is a new movement in the criminal justice system called Restorative Justice, in which the emphasis is on the offender apologizing directly to his or her victim and making restitution as part of, or in lieu of, prison time.

5. As more and more people come to recognize the importance of spirituality in their lives, many are recognizing the benefits of apology and forgiveness.

6. Even some political figures are apologizing for mistakes they have made, not because it is politically advantageous, but because they feel it is the right thing to do.

At 77 years old, George Wallace, the man who was a menacing national presence during the civil rights struggles, did what few political figures ever do. For what appears to be no public gain, he declared he was wrong for his famous 1963 "stand in the schoolhouse door," intended to keep two young black students from integrating the University of Alabama. He confessed not to the press but to the person who deserved to hear it—Vivian Malone Jones—the young woman whom he had confronted along with student James Hood.

7. Several years ago in Los Angeles an Apology Sound-Off Line was established—a telephone call-in service that offers the catharsis of confession for the price of a phone call. They receive some 200 anonymous calls a day from people admitting everything from marital infidelity to murder.

8. More and more people are becoming aware of how important it is to teach and encourage children to apologize.

Suellen Fried, the author of *Bullies and Victims: Helping Your Child Survive the Schoolyard Battlefield*, explores the long-term effects of the destructive conflicts that often occur between children, and the grave consequences these relationships have on schools, families, and society. Noting that many of the children who are shooting other children were the victims of bullying and teasing by other children, Ms. Fried went into the schools to educate children about the negative effects of peer abuse.

Part of her program is to encourage children to apologize for making derogatory remarks to other children or for not sticking up for kids who are being bullied. During each workshop she might say, "I'm sure that now that you understand how much teasing and bullying hurts other children, you can each think of a child you need to apologize to. This will make you and them feel a lot better." Then she calls on each child who has his or her hand up. One by one, each child openly apologizes to someone in the group, using his or her name and spelling out the offense, such as: "I didn't stand up for Cindy when the other kids were making fun of her and I'm sorry."

In this way, Ms. Fried is trying to stop bullying before physical and emotional abuse occurs, as well as teaching the importance of apology. The children who received an apology no doubt benefited greatly, as did those who apologized.

My hope is that *The Power of Apology* will cause the seeds that have already been planted to bloom into a full-fledged movement. There is an interconnection between the small apologies we can and should make on a daily basis and those that need to be made by larger groups and countries. Beginning to take responsibility for our actions instead of denying responsibility or blaming others can transform all of our relationships—whether they be romantic, family, or business—as well as our culture.

Being open to accepting the apologies that others give us will help us all move from judgment to empathy. We will become more compassionate human beings—toward others and ourselves.

Asking for apologies can be a revolutionary way of dealing with our anger, which in turn can cut down on the number of divorces, the problems parents have with acting-out children, and possibly even the amount of violence that occurs in this country.

Changing the World, One Apology at a Time

As we have seen time and time again, one person does have the power to significantly change the world. You have within your power the ability to make a tremendous impact on those around you by apologizing when you are wrong, accepting the apologies of those who are courageous enough to give them, and asking for an apology when you are wronged. When you apologize for actions that are hurtful or harmful to someone else, you give him or her the gifts of validation, respect, and compassion. This is turn may encourage this person to pass these gifts on the next time he or she hurts someone.

An apology can have a great impact on someone. If the person you apologized to was touched by your apology, it can make him think about the power that apology has to heal wounds. It may even cause him to think about the people he needs to apologize to and may motivate him to follow through with the apologies.

Think about it. Your one selfless apology may cause a chain reaction. The person you apologized to may be so touched by your apology that it gives her the courage to apologize to someone she has wronged. This person may, in turn, realize the importance of apology and apologize to someone he or she has wronged. Apology after apology after apology may occur because of your one courageous act.

Now think about the impact you can have on your mate, your children, your friends, and your co-workers by making apology a way of life. When we commit to putting ourselves in the other person's place instead of steadfastly defending ourselves and our fragile egos, when we regularly take responsibility for our actions and consciously focus on making amends to those we've harmed, we not only touch others deeply but we set an example for all those around us. Your mate and your friends may not only become more inclined to apologize when they've hurt your feelings but to apologize to others to whom they are close. Your children will learn from you and pass on the lessons of apology to their children. And your practice of apologizing to co-workers and customers may just rub off on others in your workplace, making it a far more compassionate and respectful place.

If someone apologizes to you and you are able to accept her apology, she may begin thinking of other people she has wronged and about how good it would feel to apologize to them. You may even become the catalyst for a turning point in her life. She may adapt an entirely new attitude about acknowledging her wrongs and seeking the forgiveness of others.

By accepting the apologies of others, you step down from your self-imposed pedestal and admit that you are no better than anyone else, that you too have hurt others and caused distress and disappointment in the lives of others. By accepting the apologies of others, you hold out your hand in loving kindness and offer the peace offerings of compassion and empathy. You caress them with the healing balm of forgiveness.

When you ask for an apology instead of distancing from or demonizing the wrongdoer, you may be doing that person a great favor. He or she may be unaware of the fact that his or her action hurt or harmed you in any way. We can all be oblivious to how our behavior affects others, and most of us are grateful (as well as temporarily embarrassed) when we learn more about ourselves in this regard. By pointing out someone's inappropriate or hurtful behavior, you may cause that person to reassess his or her treatment of others and may even be instrumental in that person actually changing his or her behavior in the future.

By forgiving the person who wronged you, you give him or her the greatest gift of all—another chance, another opportunity to do better, and for some, even a new life. By forgiving another person, you essentially say *I know you have good intentions and I trust you to do better next time. I care about you and want you to do better. And I will do all I can to encourage you to do better by letting bygones be bygones.*

Even the most hardened criminal can be permanently changed by true forgiveness. He or she no longer feels unforgivable, is no longer weighed down with debilitating shame. Experiencing the liberating healing of forgiveness, this person may decide to start his or her life anew, vowing to make up for the harm that he or she has done to others. When a person has been forgiven, he or she is far more likely to become more compassionate and forgiving of others. He or she now knows what a wonderful gift forgiveness is and wants to pass on this gift.

What You Can Do to Help the Movement

My hope is that those of you who have read *The Power of Apology* will pick up on the various strategies and programs offered in the book and implement them in your daily lives. The following list of suggestions includes some of the strategies we have already discussed in the book, as well as some new ideas. As you read them, think about which ones you can implement in your life.

1. *Apology night:* Devote one evening a month (more if you can) to apologizing to one another for hurts and slights. See Chapter 14 for a detailed description.

2. *Apology circles:* Apology circles can be made up of family members, business associates, schoolchildren, or any other group of people who need a way to resolve issues, air differences, and promote trust and respect among its members. (More information on this option is in the Appendix.)

3. *Apology mediation:* Consider apology mediation whenever you have a major conflict with someone. For more information, contact me at:

beverly@beverlyengel.com

or

P.O. Box 6412

Los Osos, CA 93412-6412

4. *Internet apologies:* I offer this service for those who are unable to locate the people to whom they wish to apologize. You can post your desire to apologize on-line along with your e-mail address.

Then if the person sees your listing, he or she can contact you if desired. To access the Web site, go to **www.powerofapology.com**.

5. Apology strategies can be introduced and applied to various aspects of the business environment, improving employee relations and offering an alternative to employee conflict resolution.

6. Finally, if we ever expect to change society, to lower the crime rate, and to have an effect on the behavior of criminals, we must make it easier for them to admit when they have committed a crime and to ask for help. We encourage lawbreakers to lie and do whatever is necessary to avoid our judgments. We encourage them to blame others, to look for excuses for their behavior— anything to avoid harsh judgment or punishment. Because we make criminals into monsters, we rob them and ourselves of the chance to heal, to forgive, and to be forgiven.

It is ironic that what contributes to most crimes is a lack of empathy on the perpetrator's part toward his or her victims. It is this very lack of empathy that is causing us to judge criminals so harshly.

By supporting and becoming involved in such movements as Restorative Justice (more information in the Appendix), you can make a significant impact not only on our criminal justice system but in the way we all deal with shame.

Two Ideas to Consider: Apology Circles and Restorative Justice

If we could read the secret history of our enemies, we would find in each man's life a sorrow and a suffering enough to disarm all hostility.

HENRY WADSWORTH LONGFELLOW

I n the past, traditions and rituals dictated how actions that hurt other people were to be dealt with. Each culture had rituals such as forms of confession and penance, temporary (or permanent) isolation from the community, ceremonies, or physical (sometimes harsh) punishment. These rituals underscored the seriousness of hurtful interpersonal actions and had significant psychological effects. They also affirmed the community's ethical system, symbolized guilt, cleansed the offender of blame, and then invited the offender back into the community, unburdened by guilt.

Such rituals still exist in a few communities (e.g., the Roman Catholic Church and 12-step programs such as Alcoholics Anonymous, which I wrote about earlier), but these communities are the exception rather than the rule.

Apology Circles

Forming apology circles within families and other environments can serve as the communities we all miss and long to regain. Such circles can help us to recognize our moral failures while helping us avoid self-condemnation by encouraging us to address these failures appropriately.

Apology circles offer each family or group member the opportunity to say what he or she needs to say and to be heard by other members without being interrupted. Cross-talk, criticism, blaming, and judgment are forbidden. Instead the focus is on each member getting a chance to talk about how an incident has affected him or her, each member gaining empathy for the pain and struggles of other members, and on healing the damage caused by the pain-inflicting incident.

Who benefits most from apology circles?

- Families with members who have been alienated from each other
- Families going through divorce or separation
- Groups that have experienced a disappointment or betrayal by one of their members
- Groups that have been fractured by internal conflicts among members

For further information concerning circles, please read my book, *Women Circling the Earth: A Guide to Fostering Community, Healing and Empowerment.* For more information on Apology Circles or to inquire about circle training, please contact me at:

beverly@beverlyengel.com
or
P.O. Box 6412
Los Osos, CA 93412-6412

Restorative Justice: An Alternative to Shaming

Our current criminal justice systems and school disciplinary systems focus on guilt and establishing blame, and define accountability as punishment. But a relatively new movement called *Restorative*

Justice defines accountability as demonstrating empathy and help-ing to repair the harm. Apology is an important aspect of restora-tive justice.

Recent research has discovered that rather than stigmatizing an individual for harmful behavior and increasing his shame, the best way of dealing with the situation should be reintegration, which involves separating the deed from the doer so that society (or the family) clearly disapproves of the crime or inappropriate behavior but acknowledges the intrinsic worth of the individual.

Restorative justice takes the focus off of punishment and instead emphasizes repairing the harm by addressing the emotional and material needs of victims. This includes a strategy called *conferenc-ing* in which the offender and victim meet face-to-face, along with their supporters, to discuss the crime and set up a plan for restitu-tion. The conference begins with the offender taking responsibil-ity for his or her actions. Then the victim and his or her family tell the offender how the crime affected them. This may be the first time offenders are ever confronted with the results of their actions.

In 1989, New Zealand served as a beacon around the globe by legislating family group conferencing as an alternative to impris-onment for first-time offenders. Based on the Maori tradition of allowing family members to determine the appropriate way for offenders to make restitution for their crimes, family group confer-encing has been utilized by many members of the justice system and by school disciplinary boards throughout Australia, the United Kingdom, and the United States. In fact, several states such as North Carolina and Minnesota have made family group confer-encing a statewide policy.

As opposed to the current court system, conferencing provides the following benefits:

1. It provides the offender an opportunity to apologize for his wrongdoing. We tend to be a nation of whiners, blamers, and buck passers, yet we insist that our criminals take full responsi-bility for their actions even when it means they will be punished by incarceration. Even offenders who would like to apologize to their victims are discouraged from doing so by our current court system, since to apologize is to admit wrongdoing, and to admit wrongdoing usually means either jail time or a hefty financial set-tlement in civil actions.

2. It separates the person from the wrongdoing. The behavior is bad, not the person.

3. Remorse and apology are more effective in healing the damage than material reparation or punishment.

4. It empowers victims versus reinforcing the victim role.

5. It helps the offender to connect with other people's feelings and encourages/teaches empathy.

6. It focuses on problem solving versus placing blame.

7. It provides an opportunity for all involved to repair the damage that's been done. Accountability is defined as empathy and reparation versus punishment.

8. It advocates the ideas that the stigma is removable, repentance is encouraged, and forgiveness is possible.

Research shows that youth who choose conferencing are less likely to reoffend and that societies that reintegrate offenders back into the community have a lower crime rate than those that stigmatize and alienate wrongdoers.

Many family group conferences include volunteers from the community. If you would like to get involved or would like more information on restorative justice, contact:

Real Justice
P.O. Box 229
Bethlehem, PA 18016-0229
Web site: **www.realjustice.org**

Kay Pranis
Minnesota Department of Corrections
1450 Energy Park Drive
St. Paul, MN 55108
e-mail: **Kpranis@co.doc.state.mn.u.s**

References

INTRODUCTION

Editors of Conari Press, *Random Acts of Kindness* (California: Conari Press, 1993).

Deborah Tannen, *You Just Don't Understand* (New York: Ballantine, 1991).

Deborah Tannen, *The Argument Culture: Moving from Debate to Dialogue* (New York: Random House, 1998).

CHAPTER 1

Charles Klein, *How to Forgive When You Can't Forget: Healing Our Personal Relationships* (New York: Berkley Publishing Group, 1997).

Aaron Lazare, "Go Ahead, Say You're Sorry," *Psychology Today*, Vol. 28, p. 40.

CHAPTER 2

Nicholas Tavuchis, *Mea Culpa: A Sociology of Apology and Reconciliation* (California: Stanford University Press, 1991).

CHAPTER 3

Deborah Tannen, *The Argument Culture: Moving from Debate to Dialogue* (New York: Random House, 1998).

Nicholas Tavuchis, *Mea Culpa: A Sociology of Apology and Reconciliation* (California: Stanford University Press, 1991).

CHAPTER 5

Robert D. Enright, *Exploring Forgiveness* (Wisconsin: University of Wisconsin Press, 1998).

Michael E. McCullough, Steven J. Sandage, and Everett L. Worthington, Jr., *Journal of Personality and Social Psychology*, Vol. 73, pp. 321–336.

CHAPTER 9

Michael E. McCullough, Steven J. Sandage, and Everett L. Worthington, Jr., *To Forgive Is Human: How to Put Your Past in the Past* (Illinois: InterVarsity Press, 1997).

CHAPTER 10

Dannion Brinkley, *Saved by the Light: The Story of a Man Who Died Twice and the Profound Revelations He Received* (New York: Harper Mass Market, 1995).

Gail Sheehy, *Passages* (New York: Bantam Books, 1984).

CHAPTER 11

Charles Klein, *How to Forgive When You Can't Forget: Healing Our Personal Relationships* (New York: Berkley Publishing Group, 1997).

CHAPTER 12

Charles Klein, *How to Forgive When You Can't Forget: Healing Our Personal Relationships* (New York: Berkley Publishing Group, 1997).

CHAPTER 13

Charles Garfield, Cindy Spring, and Sedonia Cahill, *Wisdom Circles: A Guide to Self-Discovery and Community Building in Small Groups* (New York: Hyperion, 1999).

CHAPTER 15

Deborah Tannen, *The Argument Culture: Moving from Debate to Dialogue* (New York: Random House, 1998).

CHAPTER 16

Suellen Fried, *Bullies and Victims: Helping Your Child Survive the Schoolyard Battlefield* (New York: M. Evans and Co., 1998).

APPENDIX

Beverly Engel, *Women Circling the Earth: A Guide to Fostering Community, Healing and Empowerment* (Florida: Health Communications, Inc., 2000).

Recommended Reading

Albom, Mitch. *Tuesdays with Morrie: An Old Man, a Young Man, and Life's Greatest Lesson* (New York: Doubleday, 1997).

Brinkley, Dannion. *Saved by the Light: The Story of a Man Who Died Twice and the Profound Revelations He Received* (New York: Harper Mass Market, 1995).

Chopra, Deepak. *How to Know God: The Soul's Journey into the Mystery of Mysteries* (New York: Crown Publishers, 2000).

Chopra, Deepak. *The Seven Spiritual Laws of Success* (New York: Amber-Allen, 1995).

Ciaramicoli, Arthur, and Ketcham, Katherine. *The Power of Empathy: A Practical Guide to Creating Intimacy, Self-Understanding, and Lasting Love* (New York: Dutton, 2000).

Engel, Beverly. *Families in Recovery: Healing the Damage of Childhood Sexual Abuse* (California: Lowell House, 2000).

Engel, Beverly. *Women Circling the Earth: A Guide to Fostering Community, Healing and Empowerment* (Florida: Health Communications, Inc., 2000)

Enright, Robert D. *Exploring Forgiveness* (Wisconsin: University of Wisconsin Press, 1998).

Ford, Debbie. *The Dark Side of the Light Chasers* (New York: Riverhead, 1998).

Fried, Suellen. *Bullies and Victims: Helping Your Child Survive the Schoolyard Battlefield* (New York: M. Evans and Co., 1998).

Garfield, Charles, Spring, Cindy, and Cahill, Sedonia. *Wisdom Circles: A Guide to Self-Discovery and Community Building in Small Groups* (New York: Hyperion, 1999).

Klein, Charles. *How to Forgive When You Can't Forget: Healing Our Personal Relationships* (New York: Berkley Publishing Group, 1997).

McCullough, Michael E., Sandage, Steven J., and Worthington, Everett L. *To Forgive Is Human: How to Put Your Past in the Past* (Illinois: InterVarsity Press, 1997).

Miller, William. *Your Golden Shadow* (San Francisco: Harper & Row, 1989).

Prejean, Sister Helen. *Dead Man Walking: An Eyewitness Account of the Death Penalty in the United States* (New York: Vintage Books, 1994).

Safer, Jeanne. *Forgiving and Not Forgiving: A New Approach to Resolving Intimate Betrayal* (New York: Avon, 1999).

Smedes, Lewis B. *The Art of Forgiving: When You Need to Forgive and Don't Know How* (New York: Ballantine, 1997).

Smedes, Lewis B. *Forgive and Forget: Healing the Hurts We Don't Deserve* (San Francisco: Harper & Row, 1984).

Tannen, Deborah. *The Argument Culture: Moving from Debate to Dialogue* (New York: Random House, 1998).

Tavuchis, Nicholas. *Mea Culpa: A Sociology of Apology and Reconciliation* (California: Stanford University Press, 1991).

Zweig, Connie, and Abrams, Jeremiah. *Meeting the Shadow* (Los Angeles: Jeremy P. Tarcher, 1991).

I would appreciate hearing about how this book has affected you and how you put my suggestions into practice. You can e-mail me at **beverly@beverlyengel.com** or write to:

P.O. Box 6412
Los Osos, CA 93412-6412

You can also contact me if you would like more information about my Apology Seminars, Apology Circles, or Apology Mediation.

Although this is somewhat unorthodox, I would like to take this opportunity to apologize to anyone I may have hurt, slighted, or offended but have not had the opportunity to apologize to in person. As you have read in the book, I have been unable to contact some of those to whom I owe amends. If you are one of these people and would like me to make formal amends, please write or e-mail me, or log on to my Web site at **www.powerofapology.com.**

Index